Directing

Ducklings

Lessons taught and learned

while surviving middle school

Judy Wenger

Best Wishes
to the Public
Reading
Thanks -
Judy

Dedication

This book is dedicated to my former teachers at Cal Young Junior High School, and Sheldon High School who guided me through my "ugly duckling" stage. They cared enough to make me be quiet and listen, to complete my homework, to not make excuses, to appreciate good literature, and to always try my best. They were not afraid to tell me when my work was unacceptable, and when I was out of line.

Because of them, I wanted to be a teacher and help others who, like me, were at risk of failing. I worked harder than I thought I could because I wanted *their* approval. They pushed me toward becoming a "swan." They did not lead me. I had to be pushed.

Table of Contents   Page

Acknowledgements   7

Prologue   8

Preface   23

Chapter One   26
    Grasping the gold ring
        or
    What I learned from student teaching

Chapter Two   35
    The teaching begins
        or
    I am off to save the world

Chapter Three   42
    Painful lessons learned
        or
    Never come between two mad dogs

Chapter Four   49
    Discipline: Words that heal
    Instead of a cane that cuts

Chapter Five   61
Homework
or
The fine art of making up excuses

Chapter Six   65
Responsibility
or
Making them do the work

Side note...a short diversion   69

Still keeping at it...   70

Chapter Seven   73
Keeping records
or
Jumping through hoops

Chapter Eight   77
The importance of the teacher notebook
More than just keeping records

Chapter Nine   81
Using your voice to bend
Not to break the spirit

Chapter Ten   85
Choosing your words carefully

Chapter Eleven   90
     Learning vocabulary
         or
     What's in a name?

Chapter Twelve   95
     Unexpected creatures in the classroom
         or
     Dealing with fear

Chapter Thirteen   101
     When your student is ill,
     Learn what you are made of

Chapter Fourteen   109
     When Illness strikes,
     See what you are made of

Chapter Fifteen   115
     Parents:
     Helping them tune in or back off

Chapter Sixteen   118
     The difficulty and importance
     Of follow-through

Another thought–not really a chapter...   127

Chapter Seventeen   131
     You can go home again
     Even nearly forty years later

Chapter Eighteen   **135**
    Directing a play:
    Trying to put the puzzle together

Chapter Nineteen   **148**
    Your best support team:
    The custodian and secretary

Chapter Twenty   **152**
    Getting the parents in your corner:
    Give them a say

Chapter Twenty-one   **155**
    Another world, same creatures;
    Teaching in Harlem, New York

Chapter Twenty-two   **164**
    Stretching yourself in ways
    You would never expect

Chapter Twenty-three   **168**
    A normal middle school day
        or
    In truth there are no normal days

Chapter Twenty-four   **173**
    Teaching well means
    Never having to make excuses

Photos   **177**

Acknowledgements

This project began after attending the Beachside Writers Workshop in Yachats, Oregon in 2010. Bob Welch, a column writer for *The Register Guard* and published author of over a dozen books, taught, and lead the event accompanied by award-winning Oregon author, Jane Kirkpatrick. Bob was a constant encourager who stated that, "If you don't tell your story, who will?" So I began.

– Many thanks to Bob for his gentle yet constant prodding

–to my husband Kim who put up with my hours of writing

–to my long-time friend from middle school, Alison McNeese Purscelley who read and offered suggestions throughout the manuscript

–to Dean Rea, my editor and retired university journalism professor

–to cartoonist and friend, Jan Eliot, for creating the character of Ms. Wingit in her cartoon strip, *Stone Soup*

– to Roger Hite, for walking me through the Print-On-Demand method of getting these pages from my computer to a bound book

-to former middle school student Mary Ferris Vertulfo and her friend Joe Hughes. Mary, for her watercolor design on the cover and Joe for his computer tech support. Mary is a current student in the Clark Honors College at the University of Oregon. She also enjoys hiking, drawing, and acting. Joe is a Cinema Studies major at the U. of O. and enjoys digital art as a hobby.

Prologue

The year was 2010. It was the best retirement party EVER. I knew it would be because I had planned it myself. Sounds cocky, but actually I am just telling the truth. Having mounted over one hundred theatrical productions in my teaching career, I knew I wanted my last "production" as a teacher to also be a performance, but this time, of a different sort. I had seen literally thousands of middle schoolers "trod the boards" over the years, and for the most part, it was a wonderful experience. But this was my big finale, my swansong, my Tony Awards, my...okay, maybe I am being a little over dramatic. Not like me at all. Let me just say I was ready for a one-of-a-kind party.

I began months ahead by contacting a couple dozen former students in their thirties, forties and fifties who became professionals in the entertainment business or teachers of the performing arts. I searched the internet, phone books, old yearbooks, and any possible social media/professional websites I could figure out. I pretended to be a detective, and late into the night while my husband was fast asleep, I searched and searched until something or *someone* surfaced.

When I finally found a former student, I felt so successful! I asked them all to come back to Eugene on a Saturday night in June to perform for me. I couldn't offer them compensation in any way. No free plane tickets, hotel rooms, or even a meal. Actually, come to think of it, there was compensation. I did offer chocolate. Not only chocolate, but cakes, cookies, brownies, AND a chance once again to be with me. What former student wouldn't want to spend a Saturday night with his or her former middle school teacher? As if middle school wasn't painful enough, let's see if they might want to hang out with a teacher who is a constant reminder of the discomfort, much like putting sand in your eyes, just when you were starting to finally see clearly. It was a risk on my part, but I figured the only thing I had to lose was my time and any false assumption that I was important enough to cause them to *want* to come.

Turns out, I was not disappointed. Without fail, they said they felt honored and then immediately wanted to know who else was invited. I sensed that they needed to size up the competition before agreeing to such a vulnerable proposition. Either that or, just like in middle school, they were anxious about who would be there, perhaps recounting long-ago classmates they would rather not see again. In any case, before long, word was out and many other students were calling ME, asking ME if they could be included. For a short time, I was concerned that my two-hour show might turn into a multi-day performance fair! I could have had the first ever weeklong retirement party in history. Eugene has the long standing month-long Bach Festival and the multi-week-long Oregon Festival of American Music. I could have added the once-in-a-lifetime "Party Blowout for Judy," better known as the P.B, and J. event of the century. Coming back to earth, I also tried coming back to my senses. Reality set in.

Between the "students" who were unable to find time in their performing schedule, "I would love to come but I'm performing in Austria in June," "I will be filming on location," "I'm taking students to New York at that time," to my explanation as to why I had to limit the number of performances, it started coming together, sort of a "less is more" concept.

Once I got confirmation from them, I started designing my evening more realistically. It was to be a celebration of the arts featuring diverse talents with a little bit of celebrating me thrown in. One concern was that these adult students were living in Australia, New York, Florida, southern California, Washington, and in various parts of Oregon. They also were in the performing arts, which meant they might be tied up in a show or have a new gig just ahead of my party and all of a sudden, NOT be available as planned.

As with my other shows, I needed to prepare a program, enlist help with sound and lights, have a technical rehearsal, decorate the stage and foyer, and this time, add my plans for the dessert buffet I also envisioned, complete with a large chocolate fountain. In essence, all my favorite things put together: performing, students, friends, family, and CHOCOLATE! Oh... and memories. So many memories, sweet and tender, harsh and tearful. Memories of students lost, funerals attended, broken families, suicide attempts, runaways, police intervention, expulsion hearings. Thank God the bright memories overshadowed the others. I have far more memories of student successes, plays that taught kids to *want* to learn to read, confidence found, friendships forged, courage to perform, reconciliation, the joy of learning, and laughter. Always laughter. But I digress. It was party time and I had earned it.

Back to my plans. In short, I was used to calling the shots, and suddenly I was dealing with adults. Not just adults, but ones who had moved way beyond my grasp, artistically and realistically.

The planning and preparations became a family production in itself. As with the other 37 years of my marriage, I began with several conversations with my husband. Kim is the sort of guy who is a clear thinker, not given to "whims" or "guesswork." He is what we artistic folks call a realist. Definite left-brain. Throw an idea out to Kim and then be prepared to wait while he processes the pros and cons of the topic. Turns out he was the perfect mate for me because we are opposites when it comes to thinking things through. I am spontaneous and he is, well, *not.* He posed all the usual left-brain questions such as, "How are you going to find all the people you want to invite?" "Do you think all our friends will really *want* to spend an evening watching *your* former students instead of attending a typical party?" and most importantly and expectedly, "How much do you intend to spend for this party?" All excellent questions, and of course, I didn't really have the answers for him. I looked at him, wide-eyed, and smiled. Whatever I was lacking in answers at that moment, I did not lose enthusiasm.

What I did have was his support, like hundreds of times before when I had crazy ideas. In typical Kim style, he listened to my ideas, encouraged me to go with it, and slowly but surely, became more enthused with my planning. On the day of the party, he even solved the problem of a lack of garbage cans by borrowing three large bins for the evening, literally moments before the party. He helped in his usual quiet, never-tiring manner. Like the Ever Ready Battery bunny, Kim just keeps on going. No fanfare, no complaining. He just does what needs doing.

Our older daughter Bronwyn volunteered to provide the invitations. They were luxurious; complete with drama masks of comedy and tragedy, as well as nametags in various colors reflecting whether the guest was family, students, parents, or friends. I know where Bronwyn gets her sense of organization, and I love that we are so much alike in that department. Son-in-law Chris, helped with all sorts of computer and video concerns. I reared girls. Having two sons-in-law who love to tease while using their most capable technological brains is a world I had not known until those two gentlemen wisely married my daughters.

I knew I wanted a short video clip of moments from my shows that would be projected on the screen to begin the evening. That started as a problem because I had more than one hundred VHS and DVDs of shows. Even taking a couple of minutes from each would have meant hours of clips. Hmmm, probably too long. I explained what I wanted and just like that, my other son-in-law Dave used his talent in video production to make it all come together. He even included a surprise tribute from a student acting in New York, previously unseen by me until that evening, which provided a steady stream of tears and not just from me.

Younger daughter Heather used her decorating style to help Bronwyn transform the high school auditorium lobby with programs, photos, and posters. One large table displayed the dozen or so scrapbooks holding mementoes, photos, and notes. Bronwyn organized two of the largest scrapbooks after cleaning out my filing cabinets and desk. I must NOT forget to mention that all the help from the two daughters came in the third trimester of their pregnancies! Bronwyn was due in July and Heather in August, but their big, round bellies didn't slow them down in the least. They just kicked off their shoes and carried on. Pioneer women, these two. There were comments of, "Could you pick that up for me?" "I need to sit down and rest for awhile," and "I can't get close enough to the display case because of my belly." Ah, the promise of things to come.

Just when I thought everything was completed by my kids and husband, my spry 84-year-old mother-in-law, widowed twice and the strongest woman I have ever known, decided she would, with the help of her daughter Dona, visiting from her home in France, create not one but two Norwegian cakes called Krannsakaka. So, as if my stage production was not grand enough, my behind-the-scenes family production was epic. Even when the four dozen balloons arrived, their strings tangled like a huge plate of spaghetti and my sons-in-law threatened to cut them loose if they didn't get help immediately, I felt like things were going smoothly.

It is all perspective. Spending most of my life in a middle-school classroom can make most things seem "smooth." I was familiar with the South Eugene auditorium, having produced dozens of shows there so, it was no surprise to me that we had to vacuum the aisles of trash, remove bits of gum from under seats, and tape off the broken seats so a guest would not end up crashing to the ground. Just my luck, it would have been my mother-in-law who choose the ill-fated seat! Once the cakes arrived, the place began to smell oh-so-much better. Most any building inhabited by teens and preteens can never smell too good. Cakes make everything better.

The evening went off without a hitch. Saying that is a relative term at best. Being a seasoned teacher, "without a hitch" means no one died and there were no lawsuits pending by the end of the event. I was giddy with excitement but still consumed with being the director. I walked down the center aisle to my seat, cued the lights and music, and waited for the house lights to dim. I admired the stage "set" of two large T-shirt quilts I made from the dozens of T-shirts promoting each year's musical over the past two decades and which adorned my classroom for so many years. The special video clip worked, bringing tears to my eyes as I listened to the words of a student in New York who could not be there, express the joy she found in my classes and teaching. She said she wanted to push herself harder to do more because she knew how much I loved what I did and how much I loved my students. Her spoken words were placed as a voice-over after hearing the touching words to the song from the musical *Wicked* called "For Good."

> I've heard it said, that people come into our lives
> For a reason, bringing something we must learn
> And we are led to those who help us most to grow
> If we let them, and we help them in return.
> I don't know if I believe that's true,
> But I know I'm who I am today because I knew you...

The camera panned my classroom, showing it from full to empty and by this time, the tears were welling up, and I really wondered if I would make it through the evening. When finished, the gigantic screen automatically retracted on cue, the grand piano stayed in tune...again, remember that this is happening in a high school, not Carnegie Hall. The microphones worked without screeching, which is what so many microphones like to do, especially if operated by students. The decorative balloons stayed untangled, all but one performer arrived on time, and each performed appropriately, meaning no F-bombs, to the delight of the audience of nearly seven hundred.

My master of ceremonies, one of those special students who teachers cannot forget, arrived from Los Angeles, full of hugs and laughter. Ironically, in middle school, while possessing more talent than a whole class of students, he seldom prepared for productions like he should but relied on his raw talent. So why should I be surprised that he showed up to emcee my event in the same manner? I have decided he was put in my life to remind me that I am not in control. I just like to think I am. Like a loose cannon, he winged his way through the evening, using his natural gift of wit and charm. Not knowing what might come out of his mouth, I sat tense, on my guard, just like I did in my classroom with him in my classes. Still, my adoration for him did not wane. The highlight of his efforts and the crowd favorite was him singing my chosen theme song, "This is the Moment" from the musical, *Jekyll/Hyde.*

The dozens of scrapbooks, some musty and dusty and nearly forty years old were on display. They were enjoyed and laughed over as former students found photos of themselves in tights or outrageous wigs, adorned in one of their finer middle school moments. Nothing like embarrassing or awkward photos to really get a party swinging! The chocolate fountain provided by my financial advisor flowed, sending the sweet wafting scent over the crowd. The dessert buffet offered yummy, decadent cakes, brownies, and cookies. One could gain weight just walking in the lobby and savoring all of the calorie-laden treats. Besides mountains of cookies and brownies, the three full-sized sheet cakes displayed the names of all eighty-seven shows and classes I directed or created. Seeing all my past work spelled out on a cake, as it were, was daunting. It made me tired just thinking about it, and I was glad I was on the other side of it all. My productions were carved up and served without even so much as a blink. And they were tasty to say the least. No one seemed disappointed. I can't say that would be true of all of my other on-stage productions, but that is another story.

So, on it went. Singing, dancing, acting, talking, and then...just like that, a mere FOUR hours later, I was formally and thoroughly retired. Thirty-seven years remembered, honored, thanked, and displayed. Tributes from former students, student teachers, principals, colleagues, friends and parents allowed me to shed happy tears and to feel loved and appreciated. There was mention of my 2004 Inspirational Teacher Award presented by the U.S. Department of Education and my 2007 Eugene Arts and Letters Award.

So, how exactly did I get to this place of "The End" all of a sudden? And more importantly, did I learn anything along the way that might lighten someone else's load? The answer had to be YES! It had to be because a person should never experience all I have experienced without sharing the amazing journey. That is my plan.

In the following chapters, I have offered episodes of learning that helped form me into a respected and knowledgeable award-winning teacher of middle-school folks. I am a cartoon character. How's that for respect? Many students would think that was true of most of their teachers. Although it is not exactly one of those things you put on your resume, when cartoonist Jan Eliot asked my permission to "use me" in her strip called, *Stone Soup*, I agreed. Not surprisingly, "Ms. Wingit" (a play on the name Wenger, plus wing-it, which one sometimes must do in a classroom), is sometimes sweet, sometimes sarcastic, but always full of love for her students–just like the real Mrs. Wenger!

I'm not sure about everyone else, but I usually do not ask for the life lessons I receive. They are generally painful, stressful, or embarrassing. Those are three of my least favorite activities in which to engage. There is, however, the God-given gift of humor thrown in that makes it all bearable. Sort of a suit of armor that has helped me face so much and still come out smiling or in some cases, guffawing ridiculously.

I know there are many ways to teach, many successful methods, and I am fortunate to have been around many seasoned and successful teachers. I would not want anyone to think that I am suggesting that the advice offered in the following pages is somehow a "Teachers' Bible" of commandments. Rather, it is a compilation of suggestions and advice of what worked and did not work *for me* as a middle school teacher. Take some, toss the rest.

So, my hope for you, the reader, is that some nugget of advice or inspiration speaks to you through the following pages. It won't be all goodness and warm puppies for I had some very tough years. It will be honest, however, and mostly encouraging and upbeat. That's what it takes to survive in middle school. Whether you are a relative reading this to get to know me better, perhaps trying to understand why I spent so much of my life doing the same job, one of my grandchildren who never knew me as a teacher, a friend who can't really believe that I could stay focused long enough to write an essay, let alone a whole book, or a teacher or "almost teacher" who is trying to equip herself with her own "suit of armor," this book may help. Let's hope it does and that you didn't just waste several hours reading this memoir for nothing.

Preface

While I was attempting to survive my first few days and weeks (hours?) of teaching middle school students, I was struck by an amazing revelation:

Elementary school children are cute, loveable, eager to learn and usually appear to be excited about life. Have you ever noticed little kids who knock on your door and wish to sell you something to support their club, church or school? No one wants to buy anything from a person who rolls her eyes or stands on one hip while furiously chewing gum.

The elementary student is eager and willing to act like a little adult and to win the prize for selling the most wrapping paper. Everything is new and exciting. They are not tainted with the world's cynicism or by their private dramas that unfold moment by moment. They are what I call "Cute Chicks," those you see around Easter time. Who doesn't want to cuddle one of those?

Looking ahead several years to the later teens and early adulthood, you see the mature bodies of high school students, only months away from leaving the nest. They can handle responsibility, take care of themselves and occasionally make sane choices. They have made important life changes, obtained driver's licenses, and are deciding whether to attend college, travel or get a job.

The rolling eyes are more confident, the gum chewing has subsided, braces have disappeared, the skin is smoother, muscles are appearing and hostility often has dissipated.

Then there are middle schoolers, who may be classified as pre-adolescents. This is the feared beast of the maturing process. This is an age of being in "no-man's" land: too young for this, too old for that.

They are at that in-between age like the center lane of a freeway, not sure which way to go, and they often don't like themselves. So, they are primed to take it out on anyone who may cross their paths.

They are in the "Ugly Duckling" stage. They have progressed from the "Cute Chick" stage, and before long, will shake off the grey of adolescence and emerge on the other side as "Beautiful Swans." As a teacher, I knew where they are going, and it was my job to keep them from hurting themselves and others while they discovered the beauty and potential waiting to emerge. I saw in them a promise of great

things to come, a glimpse of the future. They were swans–
in-training.

By choice, I wanted to spend time among these
"Ducklings" and devoted thirty-seven years to figure out
these wonderful and extraordinary creatures.

Chapter One

Grasping the golden ring
or
What I learned from student teaching

There are few joys as great as finishing some task
that has taken years to complete. Looking back, based on
how difficult it is for me to finish even a small task, like, say,
brushing my teeth or making the bed, I am still amazed that I
hung in there and completed college. I wasn't a stellar
student in high school. My teachers would best remember
me as the one who talked too much or distracted others.
They liked me because I did what they asked, but stretch
myself and work at my potential? Naw, I wasn't interested
in that. There were jokes to tell and friends to amuse. So, I
spent some quality time standing outside the classroom
door at the request of my teachers who wanted to get on
with their lesson and not have some smart-aleck student try
to derail it.

Perhaps that is how I came to the realization that I
was destined to become a teacher. There was plenty of time
to think about it, standing alone in an empty hallway. I was

sure of two things: I wanted to be the center of attention and I liked people. Wasn't that all it took to be a teacher? I can imagine there were many of my old teachers who were shocked to find that I became a teacher or for that mater, even went to college.

I stayed in my hometown of Eugene, Oregon, and attended the University of Oregon. I joined a sorority and found myself involved there as well as in the theatre department. Sort of opposite ends of the spectrum in the late '60s where the Hippie movement was in full swing. The theatre department was well populated by such folks, and I found my conservative upbringing challenged somewhat by my new comrades. Little did I know at the time that those years in the drama "camp" with my diverse friends would cause me to open my mind and eyes a bit wider and to be much more compassionate toward those with differing thoughts and backgrounds to my own. On the other end of that spectrum was my sorority life where I felt comfortable and safe. I learned that these women were also not all alike in spite of the world's view that sorority life was all about partying and deciding what fashion to wear. My sorority sisters were tall and short, slender and plus size, and majored in all areas from the sciences, to math, to journalism. If anything, I credit many of those women for prompting me to study and to get serious about graduating.

I began to take an interest in my classes and commit myself to doing a good job. I suppose I was maturing a little, but I was not really conscious of it at the time. At the beginning of my sophomore year, what helped me the most was meeting a guy named Kim from Tacoma, Washington, who was at the university on a golf scholarship. This is the man I married just three years later. We studied together, and I seemed less distracted with him than when I tried to study in the sorority with fifty other women around. As the college years rolled on, I felt even surer that I was on the right track, not just with my love life, but with my career choice.

The day I got my student teaching assignment, I remember thinking, "This will be a piece of cake." Lacking self-esteem was not a concern. Then I learned more. My mentor teacher was to be the same woman who wrote the textbook that I had to use in her classes. I quickly realized that I had to not only be able to teach, but also I had to learn all I could from the text to be able to impress the *author* who was the master teacher I had heard so much about! The reputation of this woman was somewhat daunting. She routinely sanitized the desks and straightened each row between classes, wore nylons, a skirt, a high-buttoned blouse, and a cardigan each day, and peered through her wire-rimmed glasses with a stern "don't even think about messing with me" gaze. This was not what I had signed up for. Added to that was the reputation this woman had for her lack of humor and abundance of order in the classroom. What did I have at that point? I had an abundance of humor and absolutely no idea how to control a classroom of thirteen-year-olds.

And so my student teaching experience began. The weeks rolled by and this stern, know-it-all mentor teacher became someone I highly respected. She taught me more than I could have ever hoped. She was stern with me and at times gave me that look that could send chills down my spine, which meant, "Less humor, more teaching please." I learned the three most valuable teaching lessons from her and I will pass them on to you. No matter what one is taught in college, this was the real deal and I more than got my money's worth by watching and learning how to teach from this amazing educator. I like to think that I improved upon what she so valuably offered by adding some warmth and humor to my teaching style. I never did follow the nylons/skirt/cardigan style for which we are all grateful.

The most important Lesson: Control the classroom. If there is chaos, no one can learn. Kids need to know who is in charge. As much as it may seem, they do not feel safe if they see themselves as the ones in charge. Some will test you to see if they can take charge, but when they know it is you, and you will always be in charge, there is an air of calm that will permeate the room. The teacher must be the fence that surrounds the field and allows the critters to be safe from any predators. The critters will push against the fence, but finding it immovable, they will realize the safety and security you offer and be more ready to trust you in your teaching.

Here is where the personalities of the students will emerge. There will be natural leaders and followers. There will be assertive and shy ones, capable students and those who must be lead through the assignments. No matter who they are when they first walk through the door of your classroom, it is your job to not break them but to bend them into knowledgeable, competent individuals who possess more skills as they leave than those which accompanied them upon arrival. You must be in charge and use your power to empower them to be in charge of their learning. When you are confident that you have them where you need them behaviorally, they are set free to learn and become the amazing individuals you know they are.   Classroom management cannot be taught from a textbook. It is not acquired by having a cup of coffee with your mentor teacher. It must come from experience. The dreaded "E" word! Knowing you will need management skills to become the teacher you hope to be, you must head into your assignment with the knowledge that you will survive and you will become better at everything as you stuff your toolbox with experience.

Secondly: Have a sense of humor. Make sure the classroom humor is not hurtful or inappropriate and that it does not overshadow the lesson at hand. Middle school is the age at which they start to feel there isn't much right about themselves. Let yourself be the source of the humor. Do not use it on them for they already feel unworthy. My best humor came from me showing them my errors or pointing out something I had done by which they could identify. Humor is a powerful healing tool. This age is in need of healing in many ways. Somewhere, someone has hurt them and they have a tough time letting it go.

By the time they get to your class, they have experienced dozens of mood swings and it isn't about you. You are just the one who gets it thrust at you. In a sense, you are a physician with a waiting room full of patients. Here though, unlike a doctor who sees one patient and her illness to treat at a time, you have the joy of seeing them all at once, each with a different need. And you get to figure out the cure, teach them something, and do it all in a specified time before the bell rings. It can be daunting. See my point about needing humor?

No matter how dedicated and passionate you are about the lesson at the moment, in the back of the room, a hand will rise, and he will break your "teacher trance" and ask, "When is this class over?" You will feel the air escaping from you like from a balloon as though he poked you with a pin. What you must realize however is that he does not mean to be offensive; he is just speaking his mind, ready for the next adventure. This is one of a thousand times you will take a deep breath, sigh inwardly, and answer him with, "In just a few minutes. Thanks for reminding me that it is time to pack up."

I have witnessed many teachers or teachers-in-training try so hard to be funny that one can almost hear the eyes rolling and the heavy sighs are like water cascading off a cliff, hitting the jagged rocks below. The humor you use may not come directly from you if that is not in your nature. Find the humor in written works or in asking students to provide some (which you have previewed). Wherever it comes from, embrace it with caution, but embrace it just the same.

Thirdly: Remember that you teach kids, not subjects. Go to where they are and teach the whole child. I know you have the state testing coming up and they must be prepared for that plus you have lesson plans to follow and God forbid you get behind the other teachers in your subject, cohort, or team! But we are not assembling cars here. We are teaching human beings. We are the handlers of their amazing minds and they must be treated with respect and awe. Teach people, not subjects. Once you have established a rapport with your students, the teaching of a subject will follow. Do not strive to be their friend. They have friends. What many students lack is an adult who loves them enough to say, "No." Be the adult who is loving and respectful, demands their best, uses humor to encourage, and who inspires them to *want* to learn.

I have coached dozens of practicum and student teachers and most of them come into my classroom acting a little like the students they are there to teach. They usually need me to remind them that they are not there to be their friend. It is easy to get this role confused. I want them to be friendly, yet not be a friend, kid around with them, yet not get caught up in their games. It is a fine line to follow. There must be a division between student and teacher, just not a wall. Finding that appropriate place will make the difference between success and failure in the classroom.

Chapter Two

The teaching begins
or
I am off to save the world

My first job as a teacher wasn't the usual one. As if it isn't enough to begin a new job with most of one's life running in normal mode, my first job was far from home, far from my mother and her daily sage advice, and far from my world of friends, church, and family. Being newly married, I also had the experience of living with a man for the first time in my life. I always lived with my Dad and my brothers, but that didn't count. This was way different. It felt at times like it was me against the world. I was (and still am) very much in love with my husband, but learning to live with him and becoming a team was hard work at first. Being half a world away meant I had few resources to call to my aid. No mother to run to or listen for hours to me about the man I was married to, who did not understand me. Like so many other times in my life, sometimes when there is nowhere to run, you end up running toward that which is causing the anguish. I ran into his arms and we had to solve our own problems. Turns out, that drew us closer and we found we needed each other to survive.

Getting a first teaching job is no easy task either. My husband and I needed teaching jobs and everywhere we interviewed, the story was the same. "You have wonderful credentials, but we are looking for someone with experience." A voice inside me would leave screaming, "But we are twenty-two-year-olds. Hire us and we will gain experience!" America was facing a glut of teachers, so we headed back to the Career Information office, willing to take anything. I love it when I think things like that and God takes me up on it. I had hardly been outside my state and there I was, a mere two months later, boarding the QANTAS 747 bound for Australia! Really?

My husband and I landed in the state of South Australia in the smallish-sized town of Whyalla. We were 180 kilometers from the big city of Adelaide. Whyalla was home to the large corporation called BHP, which stood for Broken Hill Propriety, a steel manufacturing enterprise. Many of the students were moved against their will to Whyalla with their families who were looking for blue-collar jobs. Some were native Australians, called Aboriginals. The largest percentage was from Europe or Great Brittan. Between the change in customs, the mix of accents, and the fact that I didn't know where in the world I really was, it was the perfect way to begin a marriage and a job teaching English and drama to 12 through 17-year-olds. Perfect. The blind leading the blind.

But wait! I had a shiny new teaching certificate. Maybe not really shiny, but at least new. I *must* know all the answers because I was certified. It took only a couple of weeks to learn to NOT say I was certified as that meant only one thing: I was ready to enter a mental institution. Little did anyone know how seemingly apt that sentiment felt in those first few months or maybe even for the whole first year.

My first months were filled with fitful sleep, anxiety, and lesson plans tumbling through my brain. Did I plan enough? Too much? Can they sense the fear in my eyes? Most of the days at school went smoothly. It took a lot of getting used to being called "Miss." They were instructed from their earliest days at school to stand at the beginning of class and in unison say, "Good morning, Miss Wenger (or whoever the teacher was)." As a newly married woman, I immediately requested a change to the usual greeting. It was the 1970s and I wanted to be a Mrs. I had waited for it and wasn't much interested in being a Miss. In fact, I asked that they just take their seats, and we would dispense with the artificial greeting. While this was somewhat of a shock to them, most rolled with it, and we were off to what I deemed a normal classroom setting. So, the days flowed into weeks and the weeks into months and before I knew it, the first holiday was upon us. I had done it. I had survived my first couple of months as a teacher. This wasn't difficult. Piece of cake.

A few short weeks later, it was time to prepare grades. The grading system was the traditional A, B, C, etc. but since computers were not part of life in this part of the world or anywhere I suppose, all comments were hand written and laborious. It took days to complete the reports for all my students. Not only was it time consuming, we were not given any prompts for comments. It was totally up to us to create intelligent and insightful things to say about each individual. Having never done this before and also never having learned about this in my education classes in college, I felt overwhelmingly unprepared. I had quite a lot of space in which to write. Hmmm. Perhaps if I write really large, I thought, it will fill up the space and look like I said a lot. My best bet was to see what the other staff members were writing and how they were pacing themselves to get the reports done by the deadline.

Confidently, I sailed through the reports, writing what I thought were very eloquent comments, remembering my professor's advice to stick with two comments: one about weaknesses and one about strengths. I finished the reports with two days to spare. With conviction, I walked into the Headmaster's office to hand them to him, so happy that I was the first to finish. I may have been the "newbie" but I was out to impress. He took one quick look at them and frowned. He looked at me and asked what the date was for the distribution of the reports. I told him October 9. He agreed but then asked me why I had recorded the date incorrectly on each report. Totally, confused, I asked him what he meant by his comment. "You have written 10/9/72." "In Australia, we always place the day before the month. You should have written 9/10/72." And then the statement that shocked me more than any other, he calmly stated,

"You'll have to redo these and in two days. I will not have reports given with errors in them!"

I left his office, my arms full of reports and my eyes tearing up. Why didn't anyone tell me about that? Someone should have been in charge of making sure I knew that. After all, I did it correctly, it was this backward country that was messed up. The ranting and raving continued internally, and my tears turned to anger. As I continued my pity party, a fellow teacher came up to me and in true relaxed Australian manner, said, "She'll be 'right. Take no notice of it. You've done the hard part, now just copy it." His calm demeanor reassured me that I could survive this.

From that moment on, I learned to ask questions. What I thought would be showing weakness actually was a show of ignorance and false self-assurance. Ask questions. Ironically, that is what we teach our students, yet we are often reluctant to ask questions as teachers. And about playing the victim? Rarely does that do anything except get you a bad reputation. So, my advice is to just deal with the disappointment and move on. Remember the wise Aussie saying, "She'll be 'right." I learned a whole lot over the next almost five years about not sweating the small stuff. In fact, I learned that most of what we do is "the small stuff."

Chapter Three

Painful lessons learned
or
Never come between two mad dogs

While in South Australia, I taught in a public high school that encompassed grades 8-12. My assignment was grades 8, 9, 10 English and Drama for the five years I was there. I was told by the head of the English Department, called a Senior Master at that school, what the curriculum was and what books I would be teaching in my literature classes. Having acquired my University of Oregon English degree with an emphasis in English literature, I was most fortunate to be in a country that valued the English authors and especially Shakespeare.

One day I was happily teaching for the first time, what would one day become my most favorite of Shakespeare's comedies, *A Midsummer Night's Dream.* My class was doing all the right things. Most students had completed their assignment of their drawing of the Queen Mab speech, an active discussion was under way, and all was right with my world. A warm feeling engulfed me at that moment that I was really a teacher, and a mighty good one at that. Mind you, I hadn't taught for very long, but if there is one thing that can be said of youth: it is that one knows so much, or so it seems. I had the confidence of a mighty warrior armed to the hilt. In other words, I had my very first teaching certificate, so that had to mean I knew all I would ever need to know.

In a flash, I heard a commotion out in the hall not far from my door that jarred me back to reality. I thought little of it as it was, after all, a school, and commotions are commonplace. I tried to carry on with my lesson, but that little voice in my head kept saying, "As the adult in charge, you had better check it out." After all, I was the teacher and therefore, the Queen, relatively speaking, and meaning no disrespect for her majesty, the real Queen.

I opened my door to see two Year 12s, which was the Australian equivalent of seniors, duking it out. They were not just arguing or pushing one another. They were flat-out fighting! I had no way of knowing what the issue was or why they had decided to take it upon themselves to solve it. The fur was flying. The blows were making contact with each of them and blood was streaming from the nose on one and the mouth on the other. It seemed very evenly matched, but still, fighting in school is most certainly against all rules. These seventeen-year-olds were just short of six feet tall and sturdily built. My "new-teacher-brain" was in a whirl. There I was, with my own classroom full of thirteen-year-olds, all eagerly listening to the drama unfolding just feet away. There was no point in me trying to continue my lesson with the uproar just feet from my door. Their eyes were upon me as if to ask, "Miss, what are *you* going to do to stop them?"

I looked but did not see another teacher in sight. "Oh great," I thought, "where are the authorities when you need them?" I knew the hallway was full of classroom-rich students and capable teachers. But where were they? At the rate these two were going at each other, surely someone was going to get hurt and possibly quite badly. Something had to be done and quickly. Without thinking it through, I stepped out into the hall, my classroom door flung wide open, and ordered the two young men to stop immediately. I began with a little humor. "Hey, you two Grizzlys, break it up!" They did not! In fact, they acted as though they didn't even hear what I said! Possible they did not understand what I said since it didn't occur to me until later that they don't have Grizzly bears in Australia. Even so, the nerve of them, I thought to myself. How dare they not tremble when I spoke. I was the authority figure there, and if I said to do something, it had better happen and quickly! Again, I raised my voice a little louder and with absolute authority, demanded that they stop. By this time, every door in the hall was burst open and students were slammed against the door jams as if they were watching the circus come to town. Murmurs of, "Will you listen to 'er?" and "Gor'blimey, she is irate!" could be heard above the din.

At this point I should mention that I am just a hair over five feet tall. As I also mentioned, these seventeen-year-olds were just under six foot. Another point is that, as a new teacher of just twenty-two years, I was a mere five years older than they. Can you sense the impending doom here? It wasn't looking good for me, and I hadn't even made my big move yet. My inexperience, coupled with my overly acute, yet artificial sense of power was, as it was turning out, a little like a Chihuahua trying to hunt down a Great Dane.

With the confidence of King Kong attacking the Empire State Building, but lacking the actual size needed to do so, I forced myself between the two boys and with my outstretched hands on their chests, yelled at them to stop. It was in the next instant that I realized, too late, that one should never come between two people bigger than oneself. The fist and blow that made contact with my face shocked me so much that I fell to the ground. I am not sure if it was actually shock or if I really passed out. It didn't much matter at that point. I also will never know which of the two boys actually hit me. I suppose that doesn't really matter either. I was "down for the count."

What did matter was that apparently my face stopped the fight because the next thing I knew, the two boys were walking me to the office, one supporting each of my arms. There I was, suspended by the two lads and not yet coming to my senses. By the time I got there, having travelled across the courtyard, I had regained my wits and overheard the two young men begging my forgiveness with all their might. It must have been quite a sight: these two tall male students dragging the short teacher through the courtyard and all the while, sweating profusely as they were asking how I was and apologizing for their misdeeds. They knew they were in big trouble because, 1) they were fighting, and 2) they punched a teacher. Things didn't look too good for them. Not an easy episode to explain to the headmaster either. For any of us.

We four sat in his office. I was assured that another staff member was with my students and they were fine. All I could think of was that they had just seen their teacher get hit in the face and knocked out by a student. I could only imagine the dinner table talk for many of them that night. Any number of parents would ask, "What did you learn in school today?" A reasonable question echoed on any given evening in most any town. The answer, however, might have sounded a tad more unique. "Oh, nothing, except Mrs. Wenger got punched in the face by two Year 12 boys and was nearly knocked out." Now I would be really well known, and not just because I was a "Yank," an affectionate term I became accustomed to quickly.

The headmaster had discipline in mind for the boys, which included the customary caning of a slap on the hands or calves by a bamboo rod. Very unpleasant, I must say, but I was grateful I did not have to administer it. After the boys were excused from the office, the boss had some words for me. He looked sternly at me and said, "Well, Mrs. Wenger, I suppose you know at this point what you did wrong?" "Yes,

Sir, I do," I obediently answered. I made sure I used the traditional title of "Sir," hoping he would focus on my good manners and understanding of his supreme authority. My head was hanging low and subservient. "Never get between two fighting students, but get help to pull them apart?" And then without taking his stern eyes off me, he added, "Never get between two mad dogs." A valuable lesson indeed, and one I never forgot.

Chapter Four

Discipline: words that heal
Instead of a cane that cuts

I had only heard about the discipline practices in
Australia in the 1970s that included caning. That was one of
those items of information one learns about, but tucks away
hoping to never need. Corporal punishment was not familiar
to me nor was it ever used on me in a school setting as far as
I could remember. Perhaps it was okay in the long ago past,
but not in my modern thinking. I must note that it was not
used often in my school so I gave it very little thought. I also
was pretty sure that teachers were never the ones who
delivered the consequences, so why be concerned about it?

Caning, in my novice understanding was the act of
using a slender, long reed called a "cane" to swat the
offending student on the back of the calves or the palms of
the hands as a punishment for misbehaving. The number of
swats administered was based on the offense. Caning was
reserved for the boys and the girls received some other less
physical form of punishment.

Almost a year after arriving at my school in South Australia, I had a young man in a Year 10 class by the name of Willie. He was cocky, seemingly sure of himself, and he would flip his head to the side ever so often to move the long red hair from his eyes. He was handsome in a rugged sort of way, and his athletic body looked almost too mature in his schoolboy uniform of grey slacks, grey shirt, green sweater and stripped green and grey tie, which he rarely wore, just to make sure the world knew who was the boss of his life. I liked this young man partly because he was from Scotland and his accent was such a treat for this American to hear. His behavior in the classroom left something to be desired, however. He regularly blurted out when others were speaking or cracked a joke when I was explaining some part of a lesson. One day after repeatedly asking him to refrain from such behavior, I asked him to step outside the classroom. I slipped outside to explain why I couldn't have him talking out and distracting the others. Memories of myself being spoken to in this same manner by *my* teachers swirled within my head. I also confided in him that I was easily thrown off the lesson by his "mouth," and in order to stay in the class, I needed him to behave appropriately.

Basically, I said I needed his help in the room, not his distraction.

We re-entered the class and the lesson continued. He actually restrained himself and let me continue where I had left off. All was well with my world. In a brief moment of feeling confident as a disciplinarian, the class ended and the students quietly filed out. The rest of the week went smoothly. Obviously, Willie understood my concern and with my strong, all-knowing guidance, he was on the road to becoming a model student. This discipline stuff is a piece of cake, I thought, confidently.

My secure feeling vanished quickly the next Monday. The class entered and roll was taken. Willie was not there. I began my lesson and again, all was right with my world. It was not uncommon for a couple of students to be gone on any given day. So, I thought nothing of it. As I was about to begin a new topic, the door of the room burst open and Willie loudly entered. He slammed his book bag on the desk and announced that he had just come from the office. My confidence was shattered. Had he not learned anything from our conversation the week before? Why was he doing this to me? How could one boy sabotage an entire class like that?

The others secretly admired his bravado but kept themselves in check. I asked him to sit and get out his book. Reluctantly, he slid into his seat. He sat there, glaring at me. He made no attempt at all to even pretend he was going to get his books out. I walked to his desk and tapped it. I had learned this technique in my student teaching. It worked like magic for my mentor teacher. One tap of her hand on a desk and the student would sense the necessity of getting back on track. I tapped the desk again. Nothing. It was a battle of wills, and I had to win.

I had no idea why he was acting so rudely. What caused this destructive attitude? I quickly tried to think of what I had done to deserve such behavior. I thought back to the last week when we had our hallway discourse. I had not sensed any anger or frustration from him. My lack of experience did not allow me to understand what I know now for sure. This was not about me. This issue was about something far bigger than my class or even me. Still, I had a job to do, and I could not let the others sense any weakness on my part or it would be all over for me. While I spoke to the class about our lesson, I quickly filled out an office referral for Willie. He needed to leave my room, and I had nowhere else to send him than to the office. As for the reason why he was being sent, I simply wrote, "Insubordinate." I can honestly say I had never used that word in my life, and now, here it was, written in black ink on an official referral or disciplinary form.

I quietly and without any verbal interaction, handed the slip to him. I continued talking and kept Willie in the corner of my eye. He just sat there. Now what was I to do if he chose NOT to leave? My heart was pounding in my chest, and I waited for what seemed an eternity. Slowly, with absolutely no fanfare, he picked up his book bag and headed for the door. I was waiting for a parting comment or at least a slamming of the door, but neither came. He just left quietly. Willie was *quietly* gone. I had restored order in my classroom, yet I felt strangely unsure that I had done the correct thing. Had I followed protocol? Did I give him ample warning about my expectations? What if I was too quick to call him out and he didn't really understand my requests? I tried with all my might to carry on as though nothing had happened.

Within a few minutes, the assistant headmaster arrived at my room. My heart beat loudly as he walked over to me. He whispered to me that I was to head to the office to discuss Willie and he would supervise the end of the class. Just like that, I was off to the office on official business for the first time in my teaching career. It seemed like a long walk from my building, across the courtyard, and into the main building. Thoughts raced through my head. Did I do the right thing? Did I follow protocol for disciplinary issues? Maybe I was the one who was going to be in trouble. Yes, I was certain of it.

I was met by the headmaster, a middle aged man in a suit and tie. His short, slightly graying hair was trimmed precisely. His furrowed brow indicated his angst at what was to follow. He called me into the outer office for a short discussion. Willie was sitting in his office. The headmaster, a serious man, explained to me that Willie had a history of talking out and generally not following school policy. I was not the only teacher who was having difficulty with him. I was, however, the one who had sent him to the office, and now, I had to deal with it.

It was at that moment, learning what I was to do, that I nearly decided right then to resign from my job. I was to cane the young man! Cane him! Hit him! My head was swirling with emotion. I asked the headmaster why I was to do that as I thought caning was always up to the headmaster. He responded that he had caned him just recently and now, Willie needed to get his consequence from a teacher. Naively, I asked if there was perhaps a better form of discipline for him. I may have been young, but I was not stupid. In a matter of seconds, I found myself being glared at and scolded by my boss. How dare I question his request? I gathered that teachers just knew they were never to question the headmaster. I was to do what he asked or face my own consequence.

I swallowed hard. With the headmaster watching my every move, he handed me the cane and directed me to his office door. Behind that door was an adolescent who was in trouble. His immediate fate lay in my hands and in just a few seconds I was to administer three swats of the cane to his hands. I felt sick to my stomach. Remembering the incident where I was cuffed by the two larger students, this seemed far more significant. I would rather be hurt than hurt others. With the eyes of the headmaster burning a hole into my back, I moved forward.

I opened the door and walked in. Willie was sitting in the straight-backed wooden chair with his head hanging on his chest and his hands in his lap. He didn't even look up when I entered. I looked at Willie. Could he hear the loud thumping in my chest? My mind was trying to conjure up just how I got to this spot. It was then that I had a revelation. It occurred to me that I didn't know anything about this boy. I had absolutely no information about his background. Something inside me screamed, "STOP!" I slowly closed the door and as it latched, I am sure I heard the heavy sound of a prison door clanking. Willie did not move.

With my heart pounding, I moved over beside him and sat down. The seconds ticked by, and I prayed for strength. I was not prepared in college for this event. I had a job to do and this was supposedly part of it. As I silently prayed for help, eyes open and searching for answers, I suddenly knew what I was to do. Knowing the headmaster was just outside, I quietly whispered to the boy. "Willie, I do not want to do this to you. I felt I had to send you out of the room because you were taking my lesson away from the rest of the students who were there to learn. I had to carry on with the lesson. I just want to know why you are so angry with me? Can you help me learn what I have done to upset you so?" He looked up at me, silently. I could see that he had been crying. There were still tears staining his freckled, tanned skin. "Why do you care what I think or why I act like I do?" he mumbled to me. "Just cane me, and let me out of here."

It was at that moment that I made my decision. I could not cane him. If it meant I lost my job, then it was meant to be. I looked at him and said, "Willie, I am not going to cane you. Please understand that I have been ordered to do so. I need you to help me here. I want you to cry out as though I have, but all I really want from you is to understand that I am trying to teach. I am new to teaching, and new to your country. I need you to *help* me be a good teacher. I want you to help me and in exchange, I will teach you what you need to know about literature. So here is my plan. When I slap the desk with this cane, you will cry out. Then you will leave this room. If you choose to tell anyone that I didn't really cane you, I will most likely lose my job. If that is what you want, then you know what to do. I am hoping you will walk out of here with a new understanding of the roles we both have. If you will give me another chance, I will do the same for you."

That was all he needed: another chance. He also needed to feel he had some power and he did. He never mentioned what went on in the headmaster's office that day. Or if he did, I never heard about it. In a sense, we both needed a fresh start, and we both gave each other one. Willie became one of my prized students, passing beautifully and even starring in a play.

I learned that day that real power sometimes comes in the form of meekness. We all need second chances, and sometimes a third or fourth. Kids need the teacher to model the behavior expected of the student. I showed Willie that I valued him as a human being. I also modeled my own weakness and gave him the power to help me. It was a long shot to trust him, but one I was willing to take. I found myself taking those chances hundreds of times during the next thirty-plus years. I don't regret ANY one of them.

Teaching in Australia turned out to be a wonderful experience. Our two-year commitment turned into five. We couldn't have hoped for a better situation, even if our time there began with a month-long stay in a motel because there wasn't a house for us. Even with my ectopic pregnancy and weeklong stay in the hospital and the seven pints of blood I was given after a massive hemorrhage. Yes, even after dealing with my Red-Back spider bite that caused my leg to become numb for several days. The friends we made turned out to be those lifetime-type friends who take you in and never really let you go. The easy charm and friendly attitude made for people who grabbed your heart and made you *want* to stay.

I am happy we took the opportunity to travel to a place we knew nothing about. It was there that we gained teaching experience. I loved my teaching more than I ever imagined and Kim, well, did not. He was quite happy to be going home, simply to get out of the classroom. Home to new possibilities and hopefully a new career. Just what that career would be was completely unknown to us. I was pregnant with our first child so I *knew* what I would be doing. Kim? He wanted to work on a golf course. Of course he did. He was an excellent golfer and really did not want to be in a classroom with dozens of young people. That, however, is another story. Suffice it to say he got his wish, I got mine, and we both got ours in the form of a baby daughter named

Bronwyn. We decided on the name because it was so popular in my classes. It was not uncommon to have at least two or three Bronwyn's in a class. Again, I digress. We came home to our old life, but this time as experienced teachers about to begin raising a family. If I get started writing about my children, I will never get back to the subject of this memoir about teaching. My family is the only thing on this earth I love more than teaching. Enough said. So how did I end up in a middle school? Why not make the natural progression to teaching high school or going into administration? I believe middle school chose me. Even after taking graduate courses to gain my administration certificate, I choose to remain as a teacher. An opening came up, I got a phone call, and the rest is history, or in my case, a delightful musical!

Chapter Five

Homework
or
The fine art of making up excuses

Homework in middle school is akin to asking a student to pour burning hot oil in his eye or take out the garbage. Not likely to happen, given normal circumstances. While we could all agree that homework is a necessary part of learning, how it is administered and handled is of the utmost importance. Assigning homework because you are the teacher and it seems like a good idea probably isn't. Let's look at the psychology of homework.

When you get home at the end of your day, there are certain tasks that must be completed. There is no getting around it. Some jobs must happen or something else can't happen. It is all part of that "natural consequence" part of life. If you don't empty the overfull garbage, it will become stinky or spill onto the floor. If you don't wash the dishes, eventually you will not have any clean ones left. If you don't buy more toilet paper, one day you will wish you had. The point here is that, as adults, we just know what needs to be done. We have learned by our mistakes or through repetitive "trial and error" experience that there is a better, efficient way to do things. Homework is like that.

I have long felt that for homework to be justified for the student, teachers must know why we are assigning it. We must be realistic about the time it will take a student to complete it, and when it is completed, we need to know why it was important to do. We have all experienced the pain of having homework assigned as "busy-work" or ill-explained work that we take home, only to find that we are confused or frustrated at the task. Nothing brands a student's emotional psyche as a failure like homework that is too complicated or time-consuming. Following are my suggestions for getting students to successfully complete homework on a consistent basis. I didn't start out with these ideas, but they came together once I sensed the deplorable state of the "H" word.

1. Begin the homework assignment in class. Never send the student home with a blank page. If the work has begun in class and you are confident the student understands where the assignment is going, you are likely to see the completed work in class. This is the

correct time to check understanding and to redirect the student if needed.

2. Be realistic about the time needed to complete the task. It is better to assign less and have it done well than to assign too much and have it done poorly or not at all.

3. Make sure the homework is used as a bridge between two relevant experiences. If the homework is a necessity in to progress to the next step, the student is more likely to realize the need to stay with it.

4. Never disregard the homework. If you said it is due on a certain day, then make sure you follow through. Collect it, go over it, or do something with it so the student views it as necessary to complete. If you want the class to value your assigned work, you must place VALUE on it as well.

5. Finally, I always used a recording system that all but ended the lack of homework from reluctant students. I called roll and asked each to hold up their homework to show me as I recorded the result. Students with nothing to show were penalized by not getting to participate in the next "exciting" class work.

Instead, they had to work on their missing work. Before long, those students didn't want to miss out and to endure embarrassment.

With these seemingly simple tips, you may find the task of assigning and collecting homework more agreeable and successful.

Chapter Six

Giving responsibility
or
Making them do the work

It didn't take many years of teaching before I realized a solid truth. One can't learn something without experiencing it in some form. Responsibility can't be absorbed from a textbook. It must be presented, used, and repeated. If we want our students to be more responsible, we must give them the chance to learn and experiment with all sorts of responsibility, big and small. Yet, what is it that teachers are so good at? Having responsibility. Being the organizers and planners. Taking charge. What about *giving* responsibility to others?

So, the task is clear. Give the students responsibility. I don't mean in the sense of completing their homework. Let them actually DO something that matters in a much larger picture. Let them plan an event and assign tasks to others. Let them prepare invitations, posters, food, and anything else that would make the event a success. It is with this newfound job that they can feel accomplished or learn from their mistakes.

For many years I had the joy of ending each term with an evening "celebration," culminating the end of a unit of study. I organized a Greek Festival following the mythology unit. A Medieval Feast ended the unit on the middle ages. The evenings were student directed and consisted of Greek food or my famous soup with trenchers (day-old crusty bread used as their plates, then dipped in the soup and eaten), student-created costumes, student performances, student artwork, and student set-up and clean up. No adults except for me are present or invited. I sit like a queen that evening and enjoy the food and entertainment. I give the responsibility to the students, and they run with it. Generally, some trip and fall, but the learning that takes place is well worth the race.

To be honest, it is a lot of work handing out responsibility. It takes effort to give up doing something you do well so others can have the responsibility of perhaps doing it poorly. I don't think I am selling this concept very well, but the point here is that one must have an opportunity to be responsible to get good at it. Nothing can be practiced and perfected if the opportunity never presents itself.

I have always felt that if the teacher were doing more work than the student, something was wrong with the picture. No student was allowed to leave my classroom until materials were put where they belonged and there was complete order and silence. I adopted the Three Musketeers motto, "All for one and one for all!" That "one" was actually me, but I never explained that to them. In caring for the total child, I wanted to be sure they were responsible for all aspects of the room and their involvement within that room. When a student sat like a blob and didn't get up to help, I prompted that student with the statement, "We will all leave together. If you choose NOT to help, just know that you were part of the reason you didn't leave on time. It always worked. I am not sure why. My guess is that they were usually eager to move on to their next victim... I mean class.

The best thing about responsibility is that anyone can have it. Regardless of aptitude, all students can be given a task wherein they can show success and feel proud. The worst thing about giving responsibility is that it means YOU must give up some power and allow others the chance to have it.

So, while it is sometimes easier to just get the job done yourself and get it done exactly as you want, making yourself let go and allowing others to practice learning the skill is commendable and necessary.

Side note...a short diversion...

The first persons to hear me read my early chapters of this memoir when there were only about nine chapters were two retired nurses who were sitting with me in a motel room in Ashland, Oregon. We had attended the 2011 Oregon Shakespeare Festival production of Moliere's *The Imaginary Invalid* and these two nurse friends had laughed themselves senseless the night before. As each scene of nurses, doctors, and medical equipment unfolded, the inside jokes and shared knowledge (I mean- really? How many people know what a vaginal speculum is?) caused them to unwind and guffaw as only two senior, worldly, OB/GYN nurses can. I spent the evening trying to catch up to them and wished I had paid more attention at my yearly exams. Anyway, I digress. These two women encouraged me and prompted me to continue writing. It is with thanks for that and the solid memory of their unrestrained laughter that has brought me to the publishing of this book.

Still keeping at it...

So, my original goal was to complete this book within one school year after retiring. That sounded doable and well within my limited talent. June came and went and I am still not finished. I am currently on Chapter 10 with about five more chapters planned.

Yet, here I am and it's okay. In fact, it is better than okay because I am sitting here in Yellowstone National Park in July, day two, and at the tail end of a two-week, cross-country road trip with my husband. He had always wanted to visit some of the nation's parks. Me? Just give me a good play to see or an interesting craft to create, and I am happy. I am not an outdoorsy type, although I used to own a horse and spend countless hours riding her, grooming her, and cleaning her stable. My husband, on the other hand, is a golfer, runner, biker, hiker, and all-around outdoors-type of guy.

So, here we are in Yellowstone. We have seen the requisite Old Faithful. We have seen about twenty other geysers, steam holes, and bubbling pools. They are different colors, shapes, and some smell like rotten eggs. That being said, I am all "geysered" out. My husband, on the other hand, is so fascinated with every little puff of smoke, steam, rock formation, or body of water that I fear we may be staying here for many more days. It is fun to see him so excited about this part of the trip. He has gone to hundreds of performances with me during the last forty years, so now it is his time to do what he wants. I am trying my best to have a good attitude and try to enjoy all the "famous" spots in the park.

One thing I do know is that a person can't possibly see all there is to see here in just a few days. In fact, one can't see it all *anytime* as long as the "Bear Warnings" are in effect. I had heard about the dangers of bears and the importance of keeping a watchful eye, but I saw NOTHING in the way of wildlife on the first day. I was beginning to feel as if it was all a big scam, this wild animal thing. Then it happened! We were on one of the nicely planned boardwalks that takes you safely up and around the steam vents, mud holes, and geysers . As we got to the top of one such walk, much to our pleasure and my excitement was a huge buffalo. He just stood there, very Disney-like, about six feet from us. All was good until he decided to start walking toward us and came a little too close. We backed away on the boardwalk and he moved closer but on a dirt path right next to but outside of the established boardwalk! So, in an instant I was satisfied that the wildlife did indeed exist in the park. I had no desire to see anything closer than what I had just experienced.

So, as I was saying, my book-completion has been on vacation, and I have not had the opportunity or stamina to get it finished. My excuses remind me of so many of my students' reasons for not completing the homework I assigned. I didn't allow those excuses to keep them from completing their work. I did sometimes allow them to have a little extra time, and that is what I have allowed myself.

My new goal is to finish this by the end of the summer, or around the first of September. I have used up all my excuses, and because I am dealing with none other than myself, I won't accept anything less. So, cross-country trip, Yellowstone National Park, or just plain exhaustion is, in my teacher words, "tough luck," and I will now end this and get serious about the writing. Oh, look: I think I see another buffalo!

Chapter Seven

Keeping records
or
Jumping through the hoops

I was never very good at math. It was either that, or I just wasn't motivated by the *need* to be good at math. Math meant numbers, and I rarely found that to be very creative. In any case, I never realized at first how many numbers are involved in teaching. Keeping a clear record of scores, progress, stanines, and percentages is very important to most people in education, including the students themselves and of course their parents. Oh, and the STATE. Must not forget them.

So, even though I could evaluate a student very effectively by observing his progress and testing him verbally, I kept records of everything in a quantifiable grid. I kept tabs on attendance, participation, completed homework, extra credit, quizzes, tests, essays, group work, discussion, and noted any interesting observations or concerns. Yes, I figured if I were told to keep a records book, I would take it seriously. I kept a small file box with dividers for each class.

Within the dividers I had a lined note card for each student with the name, parents' names, address, phone, email, etc. I used the cards for quick notations and for monitoring classroom involvement. However, the grade book was the master vault for the records.

The best part about a Big Fat Grade Book full of more scores than anyone would ever care to see was that no one ever questioned my grading. Ironically, I taught most of my career in a school that shared the philosophy that letter grades were not in the best interest of the student. Letter grades were best left for the older students. After all, what do actual grades tell us? An A from one teacher might mean the student is in the top 10% while another teacher might say it takes 95% for an A or maybe only 89%. I knew a teacher who just gave almost all A's so the students would still take their elective class.

I always felt that in the middle level, grades "branded" students in an unfair way. My comments about math came from a series of poor grades in math, which were really a comment on how hard I tried, which was not very hard, and not at all about what I really COULD do in math if I cared about it. Grades cause students to label themselves as "A students" or "D students" rather than proficient, emerging, or struggling. In a sense, grades are a form of manipulating or bullying students to compete against one another.

Parents add to the frenzy about letter grades. They often want their child to have all "A's" without understanding that a process is happening right before their eyes and that their child IS learning and acquiring all sorts of skills, some of which are not quantifiable. Some feel if there is an A to be had, their child must have it. Some parents, I suspect, are personally hurt by not achieving an A since *they, not their student* worked so hard for it all term, doing way more for their child than they should and redoing work their child did that was not up to the parent's standard. So, when the grades appear, some parents take offence that their work was not the best. PULEEEZE!! I will say it again. We are not assembling cars here, and we need to look at the individual human being to assess growth, ability, and drive. Many young people need to mature and realize the need for what is being taught. Of course any concerned parent wants their child to achieve success and not fall behind his or her peers. This is understandable, yet could be alleviated by less emphasis on grades and more on the growth of the individual.

Wow! My A.D.D. has really dismantled my intent to write about record keeping! As I was saying, or intending to say, there is nothing wrong with record keeping. I agree that it is important. Equally important, however, is being aware of the needs of the individual and checking all other factors involving learning. This would include checking eyesight, nutrition, social, and special awareness. Test scores from a written test are a small measure of the learning that is taking place.

Chapter Eight

The Importance of the teacher notebook:
More than just keeping records

It isn't everyday that you find the police at your classroom door requesting to take a student out of your room-in handcuffs. In fact, in thirty-seven years, it happened only once. That was enough.

Richard was one of the rough boys in my Year 11 English class in Australia. His attendance was spotty and his work reflected that. He was not a bad kid, but he definitely had some issues with school, with his parents, with life itself. It was even more amazing that I had convinced him to audition for a play and that he agreed. I always have felt that the arts can make the difference between a student succeeding or failing, but I never thought it could keep a kid from prison! Because I was adamant about careful roll-taking and keeping grades recorded in their neat little rows and columns, I knew which days he was in class and in fact, what times he was tardy or had a note to be excused early. I also knew who was at play rehearsal, who had a planned excuse, etc.

On this particular day, the police escorted him out of my classroom, and I tried my best to continue the lesson. Once class ended, I headed to the office to see if I could have some light shed on the situation. I really liked Richard and was concerned about him. He was not a troublemaker. He just didn't care much for school. Somehow I didn't think that attitude warranted him being arrested. I went straight for the headmaster for information.

What I found out was very alarming. Richard was arrested on a charge of involuntary manslaughter in the death of another cross-town schoolboy the previous day. Whaaaat? Now, I know I was a young, inexperienced teacher, but I would like to see ANY teacher handle that one with calm reserve. Murder? Someone actually died? There had to be more to this story, and I was bent on knowing more.

Of course police information is guarded and not just anyone can call them and ask for the facts. I went another route. I asked the headmaster to find out some more details about the case. Later in the day, he came to me and told me what he knew.

Turns out a group of boys, including Richard, decided to acquire some beer, skip the last class of the afternoon, and head outback to have a little party. In Australia, the drinking age back in the '70s wasn't a big deal. I often heard students talking about drinking. So, hearing about Richard and his "mates" having a little fun didn't strike me as all that strange. Where it turned sour was what I heard about what happened next. Seems the story goes that the boys drank a bit, then got to messing around like they were fighting, only they weren't. They were pushing one another and play fighting. The lad who later died fell and hit his head on a rock that was protruding from the red sandy terrain. The other boys, too wasted to be serious and thinking the boy was just kidding around (images of Mercutio in *Romeo and Juliet* here...) left him lying there to "sleep it off." The approximate time of death? 5:00 p.m. I thanked the headmaster and slowly walked out of his office, stunned and in a fog. As I walked into the courtyard, my senses returned and I stood in shock.

My attention was piqued! 5:00 p.m. I was having play rehearsal at that time! Was I only imagining that Richard was present for that or was he absent? I ran for my teacher book, the one I kept such great records in and turned to the section on rehearsals. I found the correct day's

79

page and scanned the lines until I came to Richard's name. He was present. He was with me and I could prove it. Chills ran down my spine as I jogged back across the open courtyard, book in hand. I barged into the headmaster's office, explained my revelation, and he phoned the police.

Once my book was taken by the authorities as evidence, Richard was back at school and play rehearsal. He continued through the year and performed in the play. Not much else was spoken about that incident after that. I eventually got my book back and reminded myself that it was worth the effort to keep accurate records. In fact, it was a matter of life and death.

Chapter Nine

Using your voice to bend
Not to break the spirit

I can accept that folks in New York speak differently. To my Oregon ears, it sounds harsh, demanding, overly stern. Hearing the words in the street, from the cabbie, or coming from a street vendor is one thing. I like them. Hearing them hurled at children is another.

How we use our voice is important. What is the desired outcome? Generally we speak to one another to convey information, to ask questions, or to discipline. I have found that a gentle but firm voice works well with most young people. Speaking to others as you wish to be spoken to is a valuable guideline. Do you respond best to someone yelling at you or shouting abrupt orders? I do not. Or rather, I do respond, but not in a positive way. The way one perceives our words as teachers sets the tone for the classroom.

Set the tone of your classroom before the students appear on the first day of the school year. Get it clear in your head what is acceptable language and delivery. Model it.

Don't fall into the excuse for a harsh tone by saying, "I have to snap at them and yell at them because that is all they know. It is the way their parents speak to them." That is BULL!!! Seriously! Are you going to allow profanity just because it is common among youth or with some families? Your job is to model something better than what they are used to. Your job is to raise the bar and to show how an educated, thoughtful person speaks. Middle schoolers have enough angst in their day without adding abusive language to it. Many of them hurl comments or obscenities at others because they feel it was acceptable. My guidelines were so clear and free of foul language that on several occasions, if a student misspoke, the class would gasp, clearly certain that the offensive student would be put to death on the spot. While no one ever died because of misuse of language, several received the dreaded "stink eye" from me. It was reported that it was a dreadful experience and not one to repeat.

Language is that powerful tool that sets us apart from the animal kingdom. Or is it that we have thumbs? I forget exactly, but that is not my point. Especially as technology or electronics specifically take over our lives, it is even more important to teach the value of language. Teach your students how to ask questions, how to use their voices to best express what is being thought. I always placed great value on making sure my students used their voices daily...in a good way. I based all lessons around discussion and small group learning where they had to share ideas and really listen to one another to complete the lesson. Of course, this sort of lesson is difficult for the extremely shy student or the one who has severe ADD or ADHD as those folks need more structure and self-discipline is not a strong suit.

Plan lots of discussion into the class. Make sure all students feel valued and heard. I kept 3x5 note cards (one for each student) bound by a ring for each class. Each card had a student's name on it. On those cards, I could quickly make notations, note improvements, write observations, or make a note to myself about this person's unique interests or abilities. I found that the cards helped me initially get to know a student and then keep current with his or her progress in a myriad of ways.

Final thought: If we adults want our kids to grow up speaking well and able to express themselves in an educated manner, we must teach them by example and allow them ample practice.

Chapter Ten

Choosing your words carefully

There is something strange and wonderful about the middle schooler. They are old enough to have a fairly large vocabulary, at least in their heads if not coming from their mouths. They are also at that age where EVERYTHING has a sexual connotation or has more than one meaning. Suffice it to say that the adult conversing with these students needs to be very careful when choosing the words or phrases to use in the classroom.

I could probably write a book just on the embarrassing or misunderstanding of words that have occurred because of my poor word choice. First off, the adult must come to grips with the fact that he/she is not "with it" or savvy as to what the most up-to-date definitions for current word usage might be. These definitions change often so trying to be in the know is a waste of time. My best advice is to be yourself and allow the kids to laugh out loud at you. Often.

There are some rather obvious things to avoid. Any time you use the word "balls" you will get a laugh or at least knowing glances around the room. Don't ever say, "make out" as in, "Can you make out what that meaning might be?" I also learned not to say perfectly innocent phrases like, "Get a hold of yourself," or "A pen is what I prefer." If you didn't get the last sentence, try putting "pen" and "is" together, which is what some will do as if the word "penis" is the all-time most hilarious word in the dictionary.

Other cultures will have different meanings for perfectly innocent words. In those cases, one must just suffer through the experience and learn what not to say. When teaching in Australia, I quickly learned to refer to the class schedule as "classes" not "periods" because the word periods was reserved only for that certain time each month for the females.

Aussie students would ask to use my "rubber," meaning my eraser. They would use the unsavory word, "pissed" commonly to mean someone who was drunk, or ask for "sticky tape" or a "biro." It isn't any different in American culture where we refer to items by a brand name even if that named brand isn't the actual one being used. We say,

"Kleenex" when we really mean a tissue or "Coke" when we mean a soda. But I digress. My point here is to understand that words are very important and, you must pay attention so as not to distract from the lesson at hand.

Then of course, there will be the occasional misuse of perfectly acceptable words, mostly by students. After all, they are trying to use the words they know and use most often. They are not trying to cause a distraction as they use them. One such situation happened to me when I was teaching in a seventh-grade class. We had just read a science fiction short story where a giant octopus would attack ships in the ocean. It had eyes that would glow bright red as a warning that it was about to attack. Seeing those eyes was a most frightful thing to the sailors who were about to face their doom.

In our following discussion, I asked the class, "What was so frightening about the creature?" to which one young lady raised her hand and excitedly answered, "It had huge testicles." Like a beautifully rehearsed comedy routine, there was the perfect pause, then absolute hysteria broke out from the beforehand perfectly ordered class. The young lady asked her neighbor what was so funny? I immediately responded, so as not to have her suffer more than necessary. "Yes, the octopus did have giant *tentacles*." Then, since it was too late to pretend the mistake had not happened, I said, "However, eight large testicles would be pretty scary also." Sometimes it is better to take charge and move the attention to yourself, relieving the poor victim sitting in the room.

Sometimes, the teacher makes the mistake. At least, when I used words incorrectly, it was often because I let my brain speed run ahead of my mouth coordination. One such time was perhaps my most embarrassing. I had the class in small groups working on their presentations of their Greek nature myths. As could be expected, the noise level was getting out of hand. I asked for quiet and got absolutely no response. I asked again and my usual efficient classroom control was nowhere to be found. In my desperation, I made the mistake of putting the two words together that I had in my head. I was thinking it sounded like some sort of ruckus going on and I was also thinking that too many students were making a fuss.

I raised my voice (something I did not have to do often) and shouted out, "Please stop this FUCKUS!" My accidental combination of the two words came out as a most heinous word ever! Quicker than ever before, the class suddenly became quiet, then seeing my shocked and reddening face, began such laughter as I had never heard. That single mistake did indeed quiet the class from the rowdy group work, only to replace the chatter with laughter. Eventually, the class quieted and I apologized for my error. As you might imagine, my faux pas that day was the talk of the school. This is when you are happy you have a good, solid reputation so that even a mistake like that cannot really get you in trouble. For safety's sake, I did let the principal in on my classroom "error" just in case.

I began this chapter with the caution about word choice. I believe that a person's choice of words is very important. Teach your students to think before they speak. Always ask them to create a word cache before heading into a writing assignment. When the words are available to them at their fingertips, they are most likely to use great words. As for the teacher? Try to follow my advice, even if I didn't.

Chapter Eleven

Learning vocabulary
or
What's in a name?

Sometimes the teacher needs to slow down in order to help the student come up to speed. Middle school students have been consistently coming into class each school year larger and more mature-looking than the year before. Sometimes it is the clothing that makes them look older, and sometimes it is the language. I can't do anything about the clothing and the development of their bodies, but I can help with the words used in my classroom. I am not referring to the F-bomb or the toilet language as you might expect. I am referring to the language you *want* them to use.

We all use words we are familiar with and feel comfortable speaking. When teaching a new unit with new vocabulary, the teacher must take the time to explain and encourage the student to learn how to use the words properly. I can't even imagine how a science teacher tackles that task. I still can't pronounce some of the four or five syllable words used in chemistry or biology class. I don't remember even being taught how to pronounce *photosynthesis*, but that is another story. It may have happened during one of the many times I was asked to step outside because of my over-active mouth.

My point here is that for a student to embrace the material, the student must be comfortable with the words. Year after year, I encountered the same problematic words. Generally the students would substitute familiar words for the ones Shakespeare used. If only I had a dime for every correction of "wench." It would be like this. Student reading from *Romeo and Juliet*: "That same hard-hearted wrench, that Rosaline." Me: "Notice the word 'wench,' not 'wrench.' Who can tell me what a wrench is?" Or from *A Midsummer Night's Dream*, reading the line, "Ho, ho, ho coward, where art thou?" Giggles would erupt like a babbling brook, quiet at first, then growing louder and louder. When asked why that was funny, someone would always offer, "Why is he calling him a 'ho'?" It took me a while to catch up to the modern use of the word, and I told them Shakespeare was not referring to a whore or any other derogatory label.

One of my favorite examples is from that same play. Oberon is speaking to his wife, Titania. He says, "Tarry, rash wanton, am not I thy lord?" Year after year, it would be read, "Tarry rash won-ton, am not I thy lord?" I quickly would explain that Shakespeare was not ordering Chinese food. Not won-ton, but wanton, a disobedient woman. I had failed to teach the word and the meaning before we started reading. Doing so ensures a smoother reading and understanding of the text. A character is named "Hermia," but her name was often referred to as "Hernia." Titania became Titanium.

The students will bring enough of their current slang and terminology into your classroom without you adding to the communication deficit we more mature folks already share with these "ducklings." I recall a student retelling her weekend experience one Monday morning. She excitedly told me about her cousin's wedding and how beautiful it was. She then concluded with, "Then right after the ceremony, we were all invited to the conception." My mind took me to a place it should not have gone. Suddenly I was blushing and torn between correcting her, letting it go, or imagining if she was correct and this was a very kinky family. I decided it was best to save her future embarrassment and correct her. She was indeed mortified but grateful for the friendly help.

Being bold in the correction while being sensitive to the person is another way of showing how much you care for the student. But this chapter is about the vocabulary you *want* them to use in relation to the text.

Teaching literature demands teaching vocabulary. Without boring the students silly with lists of obscure words that they will soon be reading in a book they have not chosen, make the learning meaningful. Have students offer words from the reading that they either do not know or have trouble pronouncing. Make a master list and form groups of students who can then discuss and come up with definitions by reading the words in context. Teach the way to learn meanings of words by how they are used and who says them. Read aloud. Middle-school students like to be read to. They like to hear a good story. If reading aloud is a problem for some of them, do not disgrace them by making them read. Yes, they need to practice their reading skills, but it does not have to be in a setting that places them "on stage."

Give them the task of using the words in writing and verbally. Make the words relevant. I loved hearing the kids in my Shakespeare classes walking around the halls using Elizabethan vocabulary. I miss hearing kids say, "Unhand my binder, you rogue!" or "You scurvy knave, you stole my pencil."

Once the vocabulary is second nature, reading the literature becomes familiar and even reluctant students will give it a try. Words are important. Take the time to bring them to life. Your efforts will not only be appreciated in the classroom, but when these words are shared at home, parents will feel their middle schooler is gaining something valuable.

Chapter Twelve

Unexpected creatures in the classroom
or
Dealing with fear

Teaching middle school can be challenging enough without added distractions. But there will ALWAYS be distractions. Life is full of them. Teaching kids to deal with the distractions is one of the best life-learning things you can do.

Some distractions are a little out of the ordinary. I experienced a couple of those. It was interesting that my students dealt with them better than did I. One day, teaching in our little theatre, like hundreds of days before, I was explaining an assignment to an interested theatre arts class. They were their usual attentive selves and I was pleased that the transition to group work was about to begin. It was then that I noticed most of their eyes not looking at me but looking to the side of where I was standing on the stage. It was strange because it was as if the whole class was engaged not with me but with my voice coming from a spot several feet from me.

In a beat and without turning my head, I asked what they were looking at. In a calm, quiet voice, one boy said, "We are watching the two mice on stage." Now, I am not fond of mice. I am especially not fond of mice on *my* stage and in *my* class, and just FEET AWAY FROM ME! I, in an artificially calm voice asked, "So, what are they doing?" The response? "They seem to just be listening to you. They aren't really moving." And then in true middle school humor, another student shouted, "Yeah, you've put them to sleep just like you do us," to which the entire class chortled. I have to admit, that thought had already gone through my head. In an instant the class quieted, and I again asked, "So what are they doing now?"

As I finished my question, it was noted that the little critters scampered away and were not seen again. This distraction was troublesome, but taken in stride. Of course, I had the responsibility of telling the custodian later that day and leaving the problem up to him to eradicate the space of vermin.

On another day in another year, I had another distracting situation arise that involved living things not usually associated with a language arts classroom. I was teaching my yearbook class and it involved students needing to come and go to the computer lab, a short distance from my classroom.

From my position in the room, which was sitting at a large table capable of displaying the oversize layout boards, I kept seeing students walk to the open door, hop a little, then continue out the door. This went on for quite some time, but since I was busy helping students who were coming to me for help with their pages, I thought little of it. Class continued and the walking to the door, hopping, then walking on carried on as before.

Finally, my interest was piqued, and I asked the students what the odd hopping in that spot was about. I could not clearly see as this was happening just slightly around a corner from where I was in the room. At that moment I again realized how unique this age group was. Without a grimace or affectation, it was explained to me. "We are hopping over the snake that is lying in the doorway." My jaw dropped and my face must have shown a mixture of surprise and horror. "Did you say, 'snake'?"

I had indeed heard them correctly. There, lying on the floor was a coiled up snake. This was not a huge killer-python, but it was not a little garter snake either. It was a medium sized creature and it was alive. Why it stayed there during all that movement, noise, and impending danger, I cannot say. I sometimes wondered why I did. I do know that I was the only one in the room who was unhappy with the situation. I asked them why no one told me about the snake because they could have done so in the forty minutes since the class begun. Their answer? They didn't want to bother me. BOTHER ME! Really? And when did this super-caring attitude begin? I assured them that telling me that a snake is in my classroom would never be a bother! I asked if anyone wanted to pick up the snake and take it to the office. I had so many volunteers that you would have thought I was asking for a volunteer to eat candy or take the day off. I selected one "lucky" student and the snake eventually found a home in the science lab for all (but me) to enjoy.

Probably the most alarming creature I ever had in my classroom was a run-away tarantula from the science room. Now, I dislike mice and would never expect to see a snake in the room, but a huge spider? Not in my wildest dreams would I expect that. It happened one day about three days after a morning announcement that the large (are there small ones?) tarantula was missing from the science room. There was a $50 reward offered for the safe return of this favorite lab specimen/pet. The theory was that it had gotten out of its cage and perhaps crawled into the ductwork overhead. The science teacher had had this particular "pet" for a while and wanted it back unharmed.

My classroom was close to the science rooms. You know what is coming, don't you? Apparently the creature crawled from the science room to my room via the ceiling duct, decided that my room would be a great place to visit, and somehow lowered himself (parachute?) down into my room. Never again would I view my room as a safe haven. Forever after, I would be more alert and check every nook and cranny before slipping my hand in to retrieve something.

So, on that day, unknowing as to the spider-location, I continued with a language arts lesson. We were in the middle of a discussion when I heard a happy little sound from a male student near the back of the room. Without further adieu, he stood up and walked up to me. In his hand was the tarantula, actually covering his hand as it was nearly as large as his palm. It was all I could do to cover my fear and surprise. I asked him how he found the runaway, and he excitedly answered, "I was just sitting there and I felt something on my leg. I looked down and there he was, just crawling up my jeans."

Now, I realize many people *love* that sort of fun. To me, this was straight from some B-grade horror film. No doubt, I would have had a much different reaction if that spider had chosen my leg on which to crawl. I am certain it would have met its doom under the weight of the textbook I was using. Or perhaps it would have run away upon hearing the mad shrieks of terror and blood-curdling screams coming from my mouth. I was happy it was saved, and I was especially happy it chose to crawl on someone who could appreciate it. The young man was excused to take the spider to the science room and collect his reward. He was the hero for the day and the talk of the school. Me? I was just the teacher who aged several years in a split second

Chapter Thirteen

When your student is ill
Learn what you are made of

No one ever expects to become ill with a life-threatening disease in the course of one's life. That may happen to others, but not to me. So, when life seemed to be clipping along as planned, children grown and launched on their own, years teaching moving ever closer to retirement, and all seemed well with my world, I got the news that I had cancer. Not just cancer, but according to the experts, one of the most *threatening* ones. Ovarian cancer is not to be taken lightly. No cancer is, I guess. Learning that news was most interesting and in fact–inspirational. It unfolded in a strange way.

You see, I had a drama student prior to my diagnosis who had had a brain tumor since he was in second grade. He had endured countless surgeries, hospital stays, treatments and therapies to hopefully be cured or at least buy time. This boy was inspirational because he never complained about anything. While others whined about this or that, he just loved life and was grateful for each day no matter what.

If he had to miss class, he would make sure assignments were brought in completed to me or make sure I got a note from him explaining how sorry he was to miss my class.

He badly wanted to be in my play that term. Since I always "double-cast" the roles to allow twice the number of students the chance to have speaking parts, I knew I could take a chance on his health so he could have a part. The term progressed, and he learned all his lines. He did miss a lot of classes, but he always came in for extra help on his stage blocking and line rehearsal. Then, one day, quite unexpectedly, I got a phone call from his father. The boy had taken a turn for the worse. He was quite ill, and his tumor was no longer reacting to the treatments. With the performance date just two weeks away, I was asked if he could still try to do the part. Would I please not give it to the other student who was double-cast with him, but wait until much closer to the show. That seemed reasonable, and I explained to members of the class what I felt they needed to know about his absence and the plan for him to still be able to do the performance.

This amazing human being was inspirational, and I was praying for him to rebound so he could be on stage in the play. That is what we ALL wanted. Each day went by and he could not come to class. Then I got another call from home. "He is in a wheelchair now as he is so weak, but he still knows his lines and wants to do his part. Is that still possible?" My brain was in a whirl. That meant making some changes to the blocking and clearing out more space backstage to allow room for a wheelchair. Also, I figured he could not move the chair himself, so I would need to plan for another student to push him around on stage as his character needed. How was I to get him in his costume? Would he be too weak to get dressed? Would his parent come in to help him? I was obsessed with these director's thoughts. I had years of experience, yet I had never prepared for this scenario. Time marched on, and the day arrived for the performance.

I felt I had prepared the cast, made necessary arrangements, and was ready for the big night. I arrived hours ahead of the students, like always, and gave myself time to sit for a few minutes and clear my head. In that sacred moment of feeling calm and ready, the classroom phone rang. It was the sick boy's mother. In the background I could hear sobbing. She explained to me that he was upset because he was practicing his lines, and he could not remember them anymore. He knew at that moment that he could not do his part. His dream of being in the play had vanished just hours before his play was to be performed. She wanted me to know he couldn't perform and was sobbing because he was heartbroken.

In moments like these, I am ever more convinced that God makes Himself most apparent. I didn't know what to say, but God did. I found myself, choking back my own tears, but confidently saying, "If he would like to come watch the show with me backstage, I want him to. In fact, I want him to have a curtain call. He did all the work, it is the least we can do for him." His mother, stifling back her own tears, thanked me and said she liked that plan.

Much too soon, students began to arrive. Their excitement and joy for the upcoming performance was overflowing, and happiness oozed from each and every one of them. In contrast to that aura, I knew I had to prepare them for the evening. This was routine to me, but on that night, I was called upon to muster up more courage than I ever had before. I sat the cast down and asked for quiet. They could see I had been crying and immediately fell silent.

I did my best to explain what I hoped would happen for the evening. The mood was eerily somber, not the usual opening night hype. Students were worried and a little afraid of seeing their classmate so ill. At this point, they hadn't seen him for a couple of weeks and were anxious as to how he might look. I explained that he was indeed very ill and weak. The best they could do was be cheerful and warm to him and just be themselves. They seemed to understand.

When he arrived with his father, I was shocked to see how gaunt and tired the boy looked. He could not sit up in the chair so he slumped forward slightly. His eyes were sunken into their sockets, and his chemo-bald head was covered by a woolen hat. His father pushed the chair. I explained my plan for his curtain call and for his son to see the show.

The time arrived and I was about to do the most difficult task ever. All I hoped for at that moment was to appear strong and not cry as I walked out on stage with my student in his wheelchair. The curtain opened and there was deathly silence. I welcomed the parents and friends and briefly explained the few notes I needed to share, which was routine information. Then I explained why my student was

on stage with me. "I wanted this young man to have a curtain call. Usually those happen at the end of the show. He will have his now because he has done all an actor must do to prepare for a performance. I have heard him recite his lines perfectly and I have watched him move about the stage as his cues demanded. He has been a loyal and dedicated cast member. His heart is here on this stage tonight and he wanted nothing more than to perform for you. Please join me in honoring him before we begin our play."
He received a standing ovation. Tears flowed from his eyes. Mine too.

The students mustered up their courage and performed their show. They were emotional and tender. My student watched the play from my position backstage. In the darkness, I could see his eyes close and his body relax. My thoughts were all a jumble. Besides watching the script so I could feed a line to an actor in need, I kept an eye on my critically ill student. This thought kept running through my head, "Dear God, please don't let him die here like this. What will I tell my students? How will I deal with this? Please let us make it though the play and all go home soon." I realized later that I was more concerned with myself and how I was going to deal with the situation, than I was with my student. My prayer was answered as the play ended, the audience applauded, and my wheelchair-bound student left with his father. He thanked me profusely; so happy that his son could, in his own way, be part of this activity he so badly wanted to be a part of.

I never saw him again. He died shortly after. He taught me so much about living and being thankful. He taught me to see things differently, to make the most of each moment and to cherish every opportunity to do the things I love. Life is not fair and no one understood better than he. My heart was breaking for his parents and brother. They seemed strong and positive in the midst of their grief.

The school held a memorial for him the next week. It was a fitting and uplifting service with the student choir singing, several students speaking, and the principal offering some encouraging words.

I doubt that I was ever the same after that moment. I looked more intently at each student, took more time to listen to what they had to say, and laughed a little longer at the silly episodes that unfolded in my classroom day by day. I remembered my brave student almost daily. I went over that night of the performance in my head. Time and time again. I processed the feelings and actions of that night. I spent time seeing it over and over. One thing kept coming to the forefront of my thoughts, and it made me smile. He did get his standing ovation during what would be his final curtain call.

Chapter Fourteen

When illness strikes
See what you are made of

Not long after the death of my drama student from advanced brain cancer, I received a phone call from a friend of the boy's parents. He thanked me for the extra care and provision I had given the lad and wanted me to know that the drama program was the single most important facet of the boy's school life. Because of that, the friend continued, a number of friends of the family wanted to leave a gift of some importance that would be beneficial to the drama department and a memorial of sorts. He continued by asking me to choose something of value around $1,800 to be used in the theatre. I was very surprised and extremely pleased. Wow! I had never been given such a large gift and immediately began thinking of the many needs that could be met with that amount of money. Still, the man asked me to find some *thing*, as in one item.

It didn't take me long to come up with my wish. I longed for a new, fully working follow spot. This large, cannon-looking spotlight is used to illuminate an actor or two and because it is on a swivel, is meant to follow the actor as he moves around the stage. These special lights are rarely found in a middle-school theatre, or even a high school. I was asked to order the light and to contact the man when it arrived so payment could be made.

As life in middle school unfolds, the hours are fast and furious, days turn quickly into months, and the months roll by until, before it seems possible, the last weeks of school are before us. So it was with the school year that year, and the school closed for the summer before the special gift had arrived. When it did come, the custodian carefully placed the large, heavy parcel on the stage, knowing it was safe there until I could deal with it in the fall.

And that is how the next school year began for me. The year before was an especially difficult one as I simply hadn't lost many students to illness and the experience left me raw and hurting. But this was a new year, filled with hope and optimism. I entered the theatre, anxious to examine this new and wonderful gift.

I cut open the heavy cardboard box and slowly slid the object out from the box. It was then that I did one of the most foolish things I have ever done in my life. *I lifted it.*

Now, out of necessity, I have lifted many heavy things in the theatre, whether it was set pieces, props, boxes of costumes, or lights. What I wasn't prepared for was the weight of this object.

Once I had the light in my arms, I knew I could not drop it. This precious gift had to be treated well, and I had to get it to its new home. I grunted and moaned and soon placed it where it needed to be which was up five stairs into the lighting booth at the back of the room. I set it down and immediately grabbed my hurting abdomen. I remember thinking, "Oh no! I think I heard a 'pop' just then." I knew the feeling as I had had two previous abdominal hernias that had to be surgically repaired. I remember being told by my doctor that I had a weak muscle structure in that area and that I must remember to ask someone to help me with heavy items. So much for following directions. Not my strong suit!

Within a couple of days, I was seen by a doctor and scheduled for a CT scan. What I learned from that test was that I indeed had a hernia and my surgery was imminent. I wrote up lesson plans, made sure my room was in order, and made certain my substitute was ready and eager to take on my classes. I had experienced this procedure before and was not the least bit concerned, except that I was missing school.

My husband took me to the hospital and kissed me. A brief prayer and they wheeled me off for what had become a routine surgery for me. What unfolded later that day was to be one of the most jarring and incredible events of my life. Kim waited for hours in the waiting room, left alone with his thoughts, prayers, and hopes for a pleasant outcome.

Once the surgeon got in there to see exactly what there was to do, he realized he was faced with a grave situation. What he found was not just one hernia, or even two hernias, but three hernias and a small volleyball-sized water-filled cyst that looked "suspicious." It had to be removed and it had to be removed intact because the fluid may very well be cancerous. Spilling that fluid in the abdominal cavity would be a potential death sentence. The surgery grew into multiple hours and additional surgeons were called in. A quick test of the fluid confirmed what they had feared. It was ovarian cancer. Not the textbook sort, but a more rare, unusual, unpredictable type. To hopefully "get it all" they also removed some surrounding organs and tissue plus the requisite lymph nodes. Once that was completed, the main surgeon then went to the waiting room to speak with my husband.

The fear, pain, and unknowing as to what lay ahead became our life for the next few days while we waited for the lab results. Not surprisingly, my family was there at my side, and I thankfully had my students and classes to occupy my mind. When the news came, it was confirmed as ovarian cancer, but strangely, only Stage One. We were relieved. The doctor explained that rarely is ovarian cancer found in such an early stage. Women are so used to monthly discomfort in their abdomen that they usually don't give it much thought. He said that perhaps what saved my life was actually lifting that follow spot and hurting myself, thus needing surgery immediately.

My weeks of recuperation and months of chemotherapy gave me the opportunity to reflect on a lot of things. My faith had been strengthened, my vulnerability more clearly realized, and I worked hard to make sense of it all. I found myself asking, not "Why me?" but "Why NOT me?" Why shouldn't something like this happen to me? My student had struggled for years before succumbing to his cancer. I had friends who met a similar fate. I was alive and grateful for whatever came my way. And then, as though a light bulb had flashed, I saw the symbolism of that follow spot I had so carelessly lifted.

The follow spot is what I lifted to create the need for surgery. Without that "accident," the surgeons would have not found the cancer so soon. It is very likely I would have had a much more advanced stage of ovarian cancer. That gift, in memory of my student who died from cancer, was a gift to me as well. The fact that it was a light is also symbolic. It is an item that sheds light on all it "touches" just as my student was a bright light in my classroom, regardless of what he was enduring. That spotlight helped me be diagnosed, cured, and then allowed me to continue my teaching where I was hopefully a bright light in the lives of many students.

From that inanimate object, I was given life. I know in my heart that only God gives life, but perhaps he allowed that object to be used as a symbol for my life. Sometimes an unexpected gift can be used far beyond what one might think. Each of my students have had the potential to impact their world in a mighty way, just as that follow spot impacted mine.

Chapter Fifteen

Parents:
Helping them tune in or back off

Perhaps one of the biggest joys and burdens of teaching the middle-school students is their parents. If we teachers think students this age are difficult to teach at times, we must remember that it is also not the best time to be their parents. I have seen these parents screamed at, sworn at, hit, and generally abused by their offspring far too many times. Sometimes the abuse is just the rolling eyes, refusal to look at them, or laughing at them. Regardless, it is a most unpleasant experience for all involved. The immediate response from me was to side with the parents and show disdain for the student.

There is, as we all know, two sides to every coin. We teachers can't possibly know just what the atmosphere is like at home. If we ask, we will get two different answers. Because of that, I prefer to gather my parents and students together in one room and lay out my expectations and ground rules for success. This event takes a couple of hours out of my evening on one night each school year and is perhaps the best use of my energy and time ever! Of course, not all parents will come. Some will have scheduling conflicts and some will just "blow it off" as they do many other aspects of their lives that need attention. We can't save them all. Just like the story of the little girl who picked up and threw a starfish back into the ocean every few feet, we do our best to save the ones we can. Always remember, even one child "saved" is everything to that child. For that one soul, you saved 100%.

Asking the parents to attend an informal evening to learn how they can best help their student will help you learn much about what the student faces at home. I usually found that the parents who ask the most questions or who question my intentions will very likely have a student who is a high achiever. This student must do her best to please Mom and Dad.

In many cases, the missing parents are possibly not very interested in their student's education. There could be many reasons for that, so I make sure I don't come to possibly incorrect conclusions. Many of those parents found a school classroom to be very unpleasant in their past. Perhaps the work was too challenging or the teacher was not nurturing and encouraging. The fears or disinterest that a parent felt as a student only surface again when asked to come into the classroom by the teacher. As with anything we face in our lives, if we are good at it, we want to be doing it, if not, then we try to move as far from it as possible.

As your students' advocate, you get the parents as a bonus. Draw them in. Do your best to offer support. Like a triangle, you are the third side to the figure. The student and the parent are the other two. All three must work together to achieve success.

Chapter Sixteen

The difficulty and importance
Of follow-through

Teaching a lesson beyond the classroom and textbook is a difficult and heart-wrenching event. As the teacher, you are going out on a limb to reach the students with the message that what they as a group are doing is important and much bigger than just what each one of them is doing individually.

Josh was one of those students who was unique in many ways. As a sixth grader, he already was interested in girls, was an excellent communicator, and had all the markings of a soon-to-be handsome heartthrob. On top of that, he was talented in many areas. He was a natural with music, both instrumental and vocally, could move well, and could act in a believable way. He was beyond his age. With all that God-given talent, one might think he "had it made" and could sail through school and indeed, life, without much trouble. The problem with having all that natural giftedness is that for it to be utilized, it must be managed and nurtured.

This is where discipline comes in and that is, unfortunately, often NOT a natural gift.

So, it was a given that during the term of teaching Theatre Arts and directing the comedy, *Arsenic and Old Lace*, Josh would be cast in the play and given one of the largest roles. While other students were envious, Josh took it in stride. He was given a script with the instructions to memorize the lines and work hard to be "off book" in a few weeks.

Rehearsals began and Josh was brilliant. He made the class fun and seemed to be having no problem following my directions and answering any questions I would throw his way. He obviously had a keen understanding of the lines and made the humorous ones even more enjoyable with his comedic timing and facial expressions.

The day arrived when I asked the students to set their scripts down and try the scenes without them. Josh always offered to cover for any absent student on stage and to say his or her lines. I attributed this helpful nature to his maturity and of course was thrilled that he was so involved.

What I failed to realize until it was too late was that Josh was using his ability to act helpful as a smokescreen to cover the fact that he did not have his own lines memorized. While holding a script and reading the lines for the missing student, he could glance at his own lines, look up from the script, and fool me into thinking he had his lines down cold. Since I didn't catch on and none of the other students brought it to my attention, Josh continued to be, in my eyes, the stellar, helpful, mature boy who made my job easier. Because of his kind nature and congeniality, Josh was trusted not just by me but by the entire cast.

As the performance date neared, it was time for a last run through. With a complete cast present, Josh had only to worry about his own part. The play began and all went well. Josh entered and as I expected, was amazing. He really was an actor, confident and believable. As was usually the case with my performances, we ran short on time with final rehearsals and never got to complete the second act in a final run-through.

Little did I know or could even imagine in a million years, the evening of that performance was to be one of my most memorable times spent with students. That sounds wonderful until you learn that the show was awful. I take full credit for the disaster it became all because I was duped by a student who knew how to "work the teacher."

I made a point of always sitting "off-stage left" at my little desk, my theatre light securely taped down on the desk and my script open complete with blocking and lighting cues. It was my goal to always be there for the kids, hopefully making the experience as positive as possible. While nervous parents and excited peers sat in the audience, most would never guess that I was at my little desk off stage, sweating and tense, following every word, willing to help them if the need arose.

The play began and the students were wonderfully prepared. The parents were having fun and my work was relatively easy. This was exactly the feeling of success I always wished for. Happy students, happy audience, happy teacher.

At the intermission between Acts One and Two, the student actors were rushing to use the rest rooms, get a drink of water, or adjust their costumes. I had seen this picture many times and I was pleased. Somewhere in the back of my brain was a little voice congratulating me on yet another well-done student performance where the parents would tell me how amazing I am and ask, "How DO you get these kids to do this?" I would feign modesty and answer, "It must be the wonderful parents of these kids who get them to do so well." I don't know if the parents bought that line, but in some sense, it was true. Parents make a huge difference, but that is yet another story.

The intermission ended and as we all headed into the stage area, I suddenly noticed Josh sitting in a corner, pouring over his script. Jokingly, I said, "Come on Josh, we are ready to begin. I thought you'd be first on stage." And it was then that I saw it. The Look of Terror! Josh looked at me and slowly stood up. He walked over to me and said nothing. There was no cute smile, the friendly arm thrown around my shoulders that was his way of showing the world he was my equal, no joking around. He said, "Yeah, I'm coming."

That should have been my warning, but I didn't see it. I went to my desk stage left, put on my headset, cued the lighting folks to dim the lights, whispered, "Places," and we were off. The curtain opened, the scene began, and the students carried on just as they had in rehearsals. Josh entered and said his first line. As he was partway through the next one, he stopped. Understanding that this boy had almost uncanny perfect timing, it made no sense that he was pausing as he was. I cued him and he finished his line.

When it was time for his next line, he glanced offstage to me, terror in his eyes. He needed my help. I again gave him the first few words of his line, he said them, and again stopped. At that moment it was finally clear to me that he had absolutely no idea what he was to say next. The other students on stage who had been buoyed by his presence and energy on stage were starting to flounder themselves. They were clearly flustered by Josh's lack of preparation. As the show was heading into a downward spiral, I realized what I had to do. I had to sacrifice one student for the good of the whole. Josh exited stage left. I caught him by the arm, handed him his script, and with my meanest teacher look (which I had perfected years before,) told him to get out there with his script, do his part, and afterward, he could ask forgiveness of his classmates who had done their work and learned their lines. He looked at me with the saddest puppy dog eyes, as if to say, "Please, I'll do anything if you don't make me go out there."

I insisted. The other students were quietly abuzz with, "Did you see what Judy did? She is making Josh take his script onstage! Oh, my, she must be really mad! I would just die if she made me do that!"

Well, he did finish the show with his script in hand. The others brought their performing up to a respectable standard and finished the performance well. Josh did not die. He did, however, learn a valuable lesson about life. It just keeps coming at you, ready or not. When given the chance, prepare for it. Be honest and do the work. No amount of talent will ever replace hard work and the discipline it takes to be good at something. In fact, when one has been given a special gift, it comes with responsibility. It doesn't much matter what the gift is. Josh's was performing, but others have gifts of intellect, compassion, athletic ability, writing, or a myriad of others.

I must confess that I learned a valuable lesson that evening as well. Never again did I assume anything about a student. Josh disappointed himself and others that night in part because I *allowed* him to. I am not suggesting that there was anyone else to blame for his not learning his lines but him, but had I been more discerning about Josh and more aware of how he was manipulating his time in rehearsal, I might have noticed his lack of preparation. As the teacher, it was my job to test him in small ways before the Big Test or performance.

I am grateful that Josh and I are still friends. He tells me that I taught him a very valuable lesson and that he feels I did the right thing that night backstage. He said he did not feel that way at the time and was very angry *with me.* It took him years of maturing before he realized that it was a bold and loving act on my part that I did what I did.

As for me, I am happy that life lesson turned out well. One never knows for sure at the moment. Use your gut instinct and love for others to act upon what feels right. I had to save the show because I cared so much for the entire cast. They had worked so hard and trusted me. They needed to know how valuable they were and that their efforts would not go unnoticed. To have Josh use his script so the play could progress as planned, they knew that I cared about each of them.

It must be said that Josh went on to become a professional actor and is enjoying a career he loves. He has brought up that fateful evening several times over the years and he still verifies that it was a great lesson in life. I know it was for me. Now that is a happy ending!

Another thought–not really a chapter...

Somewhere in the last decade of my teaching career, I felt weary and wondered if I was going to be able to retire when I could actually afford to, not just because I *wanted* to. Then it finally dawned on me. While my students remained the same ages year after year, my body was aging and certain tasks were taking their toll on me. Climbing on a ladder, moving and rearranging desks and chairs, going up and down the stairs to the stage (Really? Only three steps?), and staying up until midnight correcting papers became an endless grind that made me question any thoughts I had about being super-woman.

Most jobs are not dictated by the age of the client. Some jobs actually involve any age of person, and some jobs of course do not deal with people at all. They deal with things. I did not want to exchange working with people for things. Still, bear with me while I whine for a moment.

Teaching a "normal" school day was never the problem. I managed to be at school early and I rarely minded staying late. It was the coming back in the evening that started to wear on me. As much as I loved theatre and special evening events I organized myself, I began to dread them and found myself dividing up the preparation tasks into smaller and smaller chunks each year, just to get through it.

My events always involved costumes. There came a time where I swore if I had to put on my homemade Greek chiton and flowing "Hera" wig once again, I would scream! My evening Greek Festival also meant ordering and picking up the Greek food from a local in-home business. I would order the food a week ahead, get the check from the office (payable out of the class account I set up where each student paid a small fee for the year's special class events), and head out after school to collect the food for that evening. Driving to the house and picking up the food should have taken about twenty minutes. But in this case, another activity had to be factored in. Tea. Just my luck, the 80-year-old mother of Simon, the man who made the food, insisted in her strong Greek way that I "Sit, SIT and drink tea!" *Every* year when I came to pick up the food. She obviously was not aware of the busy world of the teacher. She and I could not actually converse since she only spoke Greek and my Greek was...well, non-existent with the exception of the word, chiton. We sat and stared at one another, smiling faintly. The silence was deafening. I just spent six hours with middle schoolers, another two hours doing all sorts of preparations for classes, driven through after-school traffic, and in just a couple short hours I would to be back at school, in that awful wig I mentioned. The tea–black, strong, slightly bitter, and hotter than any liquid I have ever experienced, could not be ingested quickly. More time was needed for it to cool. More awkward silence. More inward stress as the minutes ticked by. As I was saying before, memories of the "tea party" resurfaced. I became weary of the extra time spent beyond the classroom. I was heading into twenty-five years of doing these events. To stop doing them just because I was tired of them was not a good enough reason. The students *loved* them. I clearly needed to retire. That way, I could quit it all and not have to admit I was tired. Their young bodies, full of energy, never changed from year to year. This time warp plays tricks on you. Being around young people can indeed keep you feeling young in your brain. It is the body that feels the years sail by. Mine was telling me to change course. I just had to say that. I would never have retired if it were about the kids. It was all about me.

Three years after retiring and I *still* miss the kids. I miss the excitement of the first day, Open House, the smell of freshly waxed floors, school photos, new backpacks and notebooks, a fresh gradebook, and the hope of a new year. Especially the hope.

Chapter Seventeen

You <u>can</u> go home again
Even forty years later

If you look at life through numbers, not something I
usually did since it reminded me of math, it all adds up to
lots of living. I got the idea from Bronwyn who created a
huge banner for my "40th Wedding Anniversary." She made
40 pennants, each one with a significant number
corresponding to some part of my life with my husband of
40 years. When it got to the fifth pennant, it said, "Number
of years lived in Australia."

We moved to Australia as newlyweds, and I taught all
five years in the same school. Fast forward 40 years and
approximately 35 of those having moved back to Oregon.
That is a long time away to still be "in love" with a place. But
"in love" I was and was beyond excited to have the
opportunity to travel back there to see old friends,
colleagues, and former students (who I cannot call "old" for
what does that make their teacher?)

We had planned the month-long trip for ages. I became very close to Facebook and intimate with email as I searched and scrolled into the wee hours of many mornings, wrote countless messages and even joined the Facebook page for my old school in South Australia where I first became a "real" teacher. I was desperate to find former students who I remembered well and who I taught for many classes or were in my plays. I was also eager to reconnect with friends who I still communicated with each year at Christmas or with whom I had lost touch. My list grew and I gained confidence that the folks there really did want to see me as much as I wanted to see them.

One student set up a dinner in Adelaide at a hotel for anyone who wanted to come. Another student set up a lunch date in Whyalla for others who could not make it to the Adelaide function. Another student arranged for me to tour my school and to see what had changed in over three decades. As the trip became a reality and as we set foot in Oz, I knew we were home. Of course, not *really* home but home just the same. This was where I learned to teach, learned to be a wife, learned to survive without my mom and dad, and learned to accept that things done differently from what I knew were actually just fine. I was and am a proud American, but everyone should have an opportunity to live in another country so they can both see there are multiple ways of having a happy life, and also to help appreciate the American lifestyle.

As the days rolled on, we saw more and more friends and students. The days were full of familiar smells and sights, tastes and sounds that first drew us to this unique place. Most of all, it was the people. Who knew that a few years in a place could be such a shaper of who I am now. Seeing my former students in their 50s who were mere teenagers all those years ago made my heart sing. I listened to their stories. Life had treated some of them well, and some wore the scars of lost marriages or children. The one constant in all of the stories was the admonition that I had made a difference in their lives. Now, I like to think of myself as a somewhat humble person, but hearing these words from them made me giddy. Had I really made a difference? Were they just being kind? I felt a deep warmth that convinced me that they were telling the truth. They even remembered things I had forgotten such as a kind word I said or a hand on the shoulder that comforted them. They recounted stories that brought tears to my eyes and caused me to blush as they went on and on about how I gave them courage on stage or just listened to them when they needed to be heard. It was those moments that confirmed once again that I had made a difference in the world. And by world, I meant just that. Turns out that "world" might just be in a country that is not your own

Chapter Eighteen

Directing a play:
Piecing the puzzle together

It is one thing to teach in a classroom with desks and chairs and another beast all together to move into an open space where the students are not "contained." It can be a little overwhelming at first. In fact, I have talked with many teachers who tried their hands at directing a play but felt too stressed and never repeated the experience. They felt it was harder to control the mob when there was not a specific place for them to be and when the whole group was not doing the same thing.

The most important thing I have learned over the years is this: it is the journey, not the destination that matters. That is sort of a cliché today and it is only *mostly* true. Of course a final performance is what we are working towards but so many life lessons are learned in the *process* that the weeks leading up to the performance are what the kids will remember coupled with that final curtain call.

I am getting ahead of myself, so let me begin with auditions. This is the moment when the kids must decide if they have the courage to really act, sing, and dance in front of you. This will either be a wonderful, positive memory or the most humiliating moment of their young lives. Like it or not, their fate is up to you. It is a lot of pressure to take on, and you must prepare yourself mentally. I found that making the audition process as painless as possible is good for everyone, myself included. Save the stress for later when the parents find out their "little star" did not get the lead role. I will revisit this concept for it is the monster in the closet just waiting to scare you. If not actually scare, it will at least intimidate you.

Make the audition private. Don't make the student in middle-school audition in front of everyone. This can wait until high school. Don't give others the opportunity to witness the off-key singing or mispronounced dialogue or (God forbid) tears from one auditioning. This is the kindest way to allow the student with reading issues to stumble over the lines and still audition just like his more competent classmates. He is *trying* and that is wonderful! Protect the student at this age and allow the experience to be a teachable moment. If classmates are not watching, then no one can make fun of the student and the student can listen to your advice and coaching without being distracted. DO NOT let the student leave the room in tears or feeling rejected. Take the time (and that can be a strain when 300+ students are coming to audition) and make sure the student is really ready to head out the doors to the others who are waiting for their turn.

Once the cast list is posted, prepare yourself for disappointed kids. While the students might be sad, or elated, depending on the outcome, their parents will sometimes project an even greater emotional state. One might think the adults would have a better grip on their emotions, but I did not find that to be true. To be fair, it was a small percentage of parents who could not accept reality. Quite often the most vocal parent was the one who had already disappointed the child through a divorce or some other life-changing event. Still, those parents consumed a great deal of my time and tried their best to get me to change my mind. Can you imagine a director telling the cast that she changed her mind and those who thought they had a part actually did not? I NEVER caved in to parents' complaining about my casting. I even had one instance where I met with the parent in the principal's office and heard her say, "If my child DOES NOT get the lead role, I will jump off the bridge!" After many hours of conversation and me stating my ideas and philosophy, I actually had to ask my principal to intervene and to tell her she was NOT to bother me with this topic again. My best defense was always stating the truth: I saw all of the auditions and therefore I was qualified to cast this play. No one else could say that. This is another reason for "closed" auditions. It certainly helps when you have a supportive principal like I did. I realize that is not always the case.

Once the cast is posted, the parents have been calmed, and the rehearsals are to begin, I made sure I was organized. First impressions are very important and knowing the play is essential. I made sure I knew names, who might need extra help, and EXACTLY what my expectations were. A quick reading of the script helped me visualize the movement and characterizations that would very soon "come to life" on the stage. This first reading always proved difficult for the students with reading issues, causing embarrassment and those glances that all kids find condemning. I used this experience to begin bonding the cast. I explained the necessity of teamwork and helping each other. I knew something they did not: while this was about producing a play, it was also about learning reading skills and cooperation. These skills would serve them far beyond the moments on stage.

I produced a calendar showing the span of rehearsals and the future performance dates. This was actually more for me, but I know it helped the cast and parents as well. On this calendar I placed dates I expected their lines to be completely memorized, when all props were to be collected and used, when costume pieces they had to provide needed to be shown to me for approval, and when tickets would be going on sale. I always asked the cast to provide a 3-ring notebook complete with a pencil tied to the notebook with string or yarn. This saves a great deal of time when the student needs to write a note or blocking in the script. I also got tired in my early years of collecting stray pencils from the stage after each rehearsal.

The rehearsal process on stage begins with the blocking, or movement. I like to move in chronological order, scene by scene, for middle-school students because it helps them see where the action is heading. Older students may be just fine with blocking all scenes with the same characters at a time, then moving to other scenes with different characters. Keep it simple and move in an orderly fashion. This is not the time to dwell on a specific character while the others have not even been on stage yet. That detail will come shortly.

Next start working on specific characterization. Ask them questions about their character. How well do they know this person? If they are to portray a realistic character, first that person must be real to the actor. I ask each student to write a short "autobiography" of the character, in first person, and answer questions such as, what are the person's likes and dislikes, personality traits, fears, joys, style of dress, and how the action of the play affects the character. I want them to see their character as a three- dimensional being, not as a figure in a book. They must agree that seeing an actor on stage must be more real than reading about one in a book. Ask the actor to begin at the head and work down through the entire body. Facial expressions? Shoulders back or slouched? Arms still or flamboyant? How does he/she walk? It is essential that the actor understand the age and health of the character as well as the relationship of his character to the others he comes in contact with in the course of the story. This paper does not need to be very long. I felt one-half to one page of notebook paper was usually sufficient.

I found the biggest problem with young actors is the voice. Often they are wired with braces and some even have "torture devices" in their mouths that make me think, "No wonder he is angry with the world. If I had to try to talk with that metal contraption in my mouth, I would be angry too."

Ask the actor to OPEN his mouth and s-l-o-w d-o-w-n. One sure way to recognize a middle schooler is by the mumbling and speed of speech. This will be one of the biggest obstacles to overcome. Do not give in or give up. I bet I have asked more students to open their mouths than dentists. There are books devoted to speech exercises. Get one. You will use it a lot and your students will benefit from it. For the audience to enjoy the play, they must be able to understand what is being said. If you can get the actors to slow down, they will find their brains have a chance to remember the lines and speak them with clarity and meaning.

It is interesting that if the students are allowed to continue poor speech patterns, they will sometimes use them long after the braces have disappeared. I always bolstered up my request of speech clarity by telling them that once they speak clearly and with confidence, they will use that skill in EVERY class they take. Adults will give them more respect because they won't sound like the typical middle schooler (of which there isn't one). Getting them to slow down is tricky because in theatre, the pace of the speech is important. The actor feels like I am giving him a mixed message. I will say, "Come in quicker with your line, slow down when you speak, but keep the pace clipping along." Huh?

One more comment about speaking. Some actors will paraphrase their lines. They will not memorize what is exactly written. This happens often with modern dialogue. I rarely saw it with Shakespeare, but with modern speech, the actor will leave words out or exchange similar words with what is written. This is a problem for a couple of reasons. First, other actors need to know their cue from the script. If an actor does not speak what is written, it makes it difficult for the next actor to know when to begin. The other reason they should not paraphrase is because the playwright has carefully chosen the words he or she wants that character to say. As actors, they don't have the right to change the speech.

The actors will want to use hand-held props immediately, but do hold off on that until they have memorized their lines and can put the scripts down. They can't possibly hold a script, use their pencil to take notes, make arm gestures AND use props at the same time. This is a wonderful incentive to get those lines committed to memory. Once off-book, bring in the props box and let them become familiar with anything they must carry, open, unfold, or pour. Remember, they are not at their most coordinated time and even a simple movement like removing coins from a purse may take many attempts before the character can do it *while* speaking lines. This is a good case for not using glass on stage also. Plastic bottles or cups will get dropped just as glass ones will. It is safer and easier to keep glass off the stage at this age. Allow the actors to use the props for as long as possible so they know exactly how they work or how long it takes to do whatever needs to be done with that specific item.

When costumes require full dresses, long gowns, or unusual dimensions, make sure you allow the actor plenty of time to practice in those items. Shoes with heels can be disastrous. I learned that lesson during an actual performance. As usual, I was behind in my rehearsals and the coordination of costumes. I had the girls bring in their heels and get into costume, ready for opening night. I had checked out their choice of shoes and approved them. I even saw that they could move well in them. What I did not do, however, was have them wear them on stage and make their exit as we had rehearsed. The result? As the girls quickly ran off stage, in their heels, they slipped. It was as if they were Lemmings, first one down, then the next, then the next after her, until all seven girls were laying on the ground their dresses aflutter and their embarrassment mounting. One girl had a bloody knee, another cut her lip, and three were crying because they were mortified. All of that might have been avoided if I had made sure they could exit quickly in their heels. Since that moment, I have never let my actors go on stage without many rehearsals in the footwear they planned for the show.

Another sad, but amusing costume faux pas was when I asked my boys to wear tights with feet in them for one of my Shakespeare shows. I had the pants they would wear over the tights, but the tights had to go on first. I made an assumption that the boys would know how to put on the tights, but I was wrong. I always asked the boys to dress in a small room and left the larger room for the girls because there were usually twice as many of them. One evening while the students were dutifully getting into costume, I heard the plaintive angst-ridden cry of one of the boys in the next room. "Judy, Judy, I need help!" I called through the door. "What do you need?" In answer to that question, I heard, "I need help. These don't work!" With my "Director's Hat" on and lacking any other common sense, I threw open the door and bolted in, ready to save the frustrated youngster. What I saw was hilarious, though not a sight a teacher *should* see in a school. There was the boy, wearing only his white underwear, bare chest, sitting on the ground, with his feet in the tights, but he couldn't get them pulled up because they were twisted several times. It was funny and awkward. He was so stressed by this garment I was forcing him to put on that he did not care if his female teacher saw him half naked! I wanted to help him, but knowing my place, I immediately called for one of the other boys to assist him. It only took a couple of minutes and the student emerged, fully clothed. Disaster averted. It is important to not put yourself in danger by helping in any intimate way with costumes. Far better to make sure you explain fully *how* to get into costume!

Once you have prepared all the non-living pieces of your play, rehearsed the living creatures and sold the tickets, you are ready for that culminating moment of the performance. I have had countless episodes of sleepless nights, anxiety where I wondered if I would survive the preparation, and many times where I had to give myself an emotional time out rather than ruin the moment with my anger or frustration. Still, once the curtain rises, the lights shine brightly, and you see the look of joy on the actors' faces, it all feels good, and you know immediately that the process and the effort was worth it. It was only during the curtain call, as my young charges were taking their bow that the tears welled up in my eyes, and I knew in my heart that

146

every second was worth it. They would never forget that moment. Neither would I.

Chapter Nineteen

Your best support team:
The custodian and secretary

When I entered my first school and began my first teaching assignment, I was nervous about contact with the principal and assistant principal. I wanted to be sure I was on top of everything and that I always looked good. Just in case one of them was lurking outside and about to enter my classroom, I always knew or pretended to know what was happening and who was in charge. As my bosses, they had great power in my eyes. They could change my assignment or write something for my file that was less than complimentary. It was only when I couldn't get my classroom door to open that I was forced to find out who really held the power: the custodian! That's right. The "Keeper of the Keys" was the one with power. He or she who has keys in a school has supernatural power because areas around schools tend to be locked like a vault. And tools? The custodian has rolling carts full of tools, and he is not afraid to use them. I can't count how many times I asked for help from the custodian, and he always showed up armed with power tools and screwdrivers of every size and shape.

Be nice to him. Bake him cookies. Buy him gift cards. Whatever you do, treat him with respect and insist that your students do the same. These folks work very hard to keep the school safe and clean, and when students treat them with disdain, it is your job to educate them about human kindness. Never make a student clean up an area in the school as a punishment. You want to elevate the custodian and his job and encourage ALL students to assist because it is *their* school. Punishment means losing privileges or time with friends, not cleaning up the school.

Be patient with the custodian for you are just one of many who may be needing him at the same time. Of course your problem is most important, but so are the other fifteen problems he is trying to correct. Remember, you are not better than he or his superior. You are his equal, but you have different jobs and responsibilities. As teachers, we often multiply the number of students we have in a class and present our need to the custodian as much bigger than it really is. He will get around to fixing it and you must be patient. Be nice to him and respect him and you will find your requests get attention before many others. The same goes for the office secretary.

This person, the secretary, is your best friend at school. She has bits of information that can help your day run smoothly. A fire drill during Period 7? She knows just when it will happen. Be on her good side, and you too will be privy to information that, even though you will always act like you don't know, will allow you to structure your lesson so as to have minimal distractions. She knows all the dirt going down in the office. Teachers by the nature of the building layout are isolated much of the day from news outside their classroom. Be nice to her. Do not demand things of her. She has a high-stress job and is at the hub of the wheel. She is a multi-tasker and must remain congenial at the same time, no matter how crazy the pace of activity. She is a wealth of information and helpfulness. She can tell you information that the student's mother shared with her which might help you intervene successfully with that student on that given day. In other words, the secretary can make you look good. Try to understand her job and the demands of her job. Some teachers think because they are teachers, the school should revolve around them. Too many teachers act as if they are the only people who are burdened and stressed. This is simply not true. It is safe to say the majority of adults in the building all vie for the title of "Most-Stressed." Bottom line: Treat the secretary and custodian with respect and kindness and you will never be sorry. You need them more than they need you! NEVER forget that!

Chapter Twenty

Getting the parents in your corner:
Give them a say

It stands to reason that if you want to teach middle school students, those students will come with parents. Once there was a time when students came mostly with two parents, usually one of each sex, and occasionally one parent, but it is different today. It is possible and not so unusual that your students may have two sets of parents, two moms, two dads, an adult sibling-parent, or grandparent-parents. In other words, prepare for far more parents than you have students. It also stands to reason that you want these adults on your side. You must see them as allies and in some sense-colleagues. Their role in the student's education cannot be minimized. Your task is to make them understand how important they are.

This is not as easy as it sounds. Some parents are emotionally absent and in no state to be the supportive adult the student needs so badly. Some parents are not even qualified to assist their offspring if there is a language barrier or a lack in their own educational upbringing. These parents will need more support-but it is essential that you invite them into the educational process. That takes me to communication.

Communicating with the parents takes time and effort. Still, all things considered, it is much easier now than it was twenty or thirty years ago. Being able to use cell phones and email has made communicating easier than ever. I remember before we had telephones in our classrooms, teachers would take turns using the staffroom phone and the extra phone in the office. It would take hours to contact even a dozen parents. Today, setting up a group email list of parents is an efficient use of your time. Many years ago, I used to visit the home of each of my new sixth grade advisees. This was a district-sponsored program, and I loved the insight I got from meeting the kids "on their own turf." I could get first-hand knowledge of the home situation, the socio-economic setting, the tone of the parental influence, meet the pets, other siblings, and sometimes even be invited to look at family albums or have a peek at the student's bedroom.

I found over the years that the biggest complaint parents often have of teachers is the lack of being informed.

They want to know before reports come out if their student is not behaving in class, failing to do homework, or not measuring up to what they know their student is capable of doing. Of course, to a busy teacher, the answer is that we prepare the reports for that very reason: to inform parents of the above issues. Still, doing what you can to nip problems in the bud is the best answer.

Chapter Twenty-one

**Another world, same creatures:
Teaching in Harlem, New York**

After teaching for the majority of my 37-year career in Oregon, it was surreal to find myself 3,000 miles away in a public elementary school in the New York City area called Harlem in 2010. I had met their teacher in 2009 at a Broadway Teachers' Workshop in New York City that focused on theatre, and we struck up a sweet friendship. She invited me to come to her classroom as a visiting "Shakespeare" expert. I hardly considered myself an expert, but I was nearly thirty years her senior, and I had taught Shakespeare for several decades. I agreed to break out of my comfort zone. Off I went to a world away from what I know. Yet what I know is kids.

> You see the same world through blue eyes
> That I see through brown
> Yet we're world's apart, world's apart
> -   from *Big River*

Kids are kids. That statement seems obvious. Whether African/American, Latino, White, or Asian, kids all need the same things. They need to be loved, respected, corrected, and reaffirmed. They need to feel safe and they need perimeters.

I entered PS 153 in Harlem at 8 a.m. and was greeted at a desk by two security officers, a branch of the police force. I was asked to show ID and to sign my name, address, and where I was going on a sheet for visitors. This is a city school, a tall brick building surrounded by traffic, ragged delis, and small retail shops. There are iron bars on the windows and iron gates protecting the front door. Everyone comes and goes through the same door. At first I thought it felt like a prison, but in a few days, it became very comforting. No intruders were getting in this building. This pre-K through grade 5 school has almost 1,000 students and some 200 staff. It is evaluated as a school on a state rubric much like in Oregon. This school has an "A" evaluation, based on school environment, performance and student progress. It is almost all African/American and Latino students with a small portion of White and Asian students.

This could have been any school in Oregon except for yet another thing. As I walked down the hall, I was stunned by the gruffness of the teachers speaking to the students. These are young students, not high schoolers and I was shocked! Comments in loud, harsh New York accents rang out, "I said get in line," "Don't touch her," "Do I have to call your Mama?" and "Don't make me come to you!" I am not saying the comments weren't warranted, but the scolding tone of the teachers came as a surprise. I know these teachers care about their young charges, and I know they are dedicated to providing a good education for them. What they don't realize is that their harsh tones seem demoralizing and threatening. It is a way of life there at PS 153 and reflects the tone of the dialogue outside the school as well. It is what they are *used* to hearing, right or wrong. They are *familiar* with the tone and apparently does not bother them. I know we all get used to whatever we have around us and learn to call "normal" whatever that environment is like. Still, it did not sit easily with me, the foreigner, and I wondered if some of their discipline issues might be dissipated with a little more respect shown through language and tone.

The teacher I was visiting was a young, vibrant, talented African/American woman originally from North Carolina. She was a specialist teaching musical theatre and dance. She only saw each class once a week. Her room was a dance studio, complete with walls of mirrors, a Marley covered floor and ballet Barres at one end. She had only a small desk for her computer, a paper bag for garbage, yet lots of video/sound equipment. She had a long, narrow storage room with lockers for costume and prop storage. The school was very clean and classrooms were adorned with student work. In fact, the interior could be any school in Eugene until you listen to the people speaking in Spanish, Yiddish, or Black "street talk." The New York accent is, of course, predominant, regardless of race.

My plan was to teach story building through Broadway music and to introduce the students to Shakespeare. Of course, only a fraction of what I had planned was actually presented. I was introduced as Ms. Wenger and the students were expected to greet me in unison. They all come into the room in a line and circled around, stopping in a relaxed but attentive manner on their marked places. Their teacher used the universal dance term, "neutral" for the cue that they are to stand at attention with their arms and hands at their sides.

It was a joy to see these multi-cultural students step outside their comfort zone and try what I was offering. Their bright eyes wanted so badly to take it in. Clearly I was an outsider, yet they had enough trust to give my lesson a try. In every class, at least one student would be disinterested and bent on dismantling the lesson at hand. Before I could handle those situations, the teacher would immediately call the student out and ask him, yes, usually a male, to remove himself from the group and sit in a corner! I was appalled and not pleased with the handling of the offense. Yet, it was not my place to reprimand the teacher. There are many different ways to discipline, and each teacher must find what works best for them. It was her space and I was the guest. Still, I felt uneasy and found it frustrating to watch these young kids cast away from my lesson so quickly. Her method was to eliminate the source of the problem immediately so she could go on with her lesson. My classroom management skills were very different. Would they work in this setting, so very different from my classroom in Oregon? I had to find out.

I spoke to my friend before the next class was to appear. I explained my objective, which was to include *all* students. I told her that I wanted to try to use my own methods of discipline if she would allow that. With her approval, I would be the one who made all disciplinary decisions. The students arrived as usual, found their places on the spots she provided and we began. Within moments, one boy in the last row started misbehaving by spinning around on his "spot," clearly wanting attention. Just as quickly, I walked to him, placed a hand on his shoulder while I continued my remarks about the lesson. He stopped moving. I did not look at him or make any comment about his behavior. The others watched with interest. I moved away from him, and he started his spinning again. This time, I decided to try another "trick." I asked all the students to get up onto their feet and begin moving. All of a sudden, my young distracter was disarmed. If the whole class was moving, that meant he could not stand out. The next part of the lesson went well. As I played various types of music, the students were to move to it and to create a character. My goal had been reached at this point of the lesson as ALL the students were still participating.

Once they had experienced that, I was ready to ask them to once again sit down on their spots for some brief discussion. Being proactive with my young charge, I requested that he sit up front closer to me. He dutifully agreed, and I found he was quite attentive. As the lesson ended and the students lined up for dismissal, the teacher caught my eye. Not sure what exactly that meant, I continued my plan. As they filed out of the room heading to their next class, I high-fived each one. When my "Spinner" student came along, I stopped him and told him what a great job he did in class. The look on his beautiful brown face was enough to make tears well up in my eyes. He beamed and said, "Thanks. You be here tomorrow?" "Yes, I will. Will you be here?" With huge eyes and an impish grin, he responded with a "Yeah" and off he went. Once the room was emptied, my friend and I sat down to debrief. She said he had rarely been successful through an entire lesson. She said he was affected by ADHD and her answer to that was to remove him on most days. I explained the downside of that and that the self-esteem of the lad was at stake. She listened.

As teachers, we are bombarded with special needs kids in our classes. Our profession calls for us to plan for many different types of personalities, disabilities, and academic levels. At best, we just hope to be able to pass along some nugget of wisdom while the student is with us. Our time is short and we must have the student actually in the lesson for our wisdom to be grasped. Having a student sit out while the lesson is happening as a punishment to the student does not make sense. Yes, it is an easy and immediate remedy, but it is not in the student's best interest.

I don't know what happened to those students I had the pleasure of teaching that one short week. I do know that I was not their only hope. Never should one teacher feel she is the only one who can have an affect on a student. That sort of mentality is dangerous and only self-serving. All one can hope is that the student who was included could transfer that warm inclusive feeling to some central part of their being and want that again so badly that it overcomes any other desire to be off-track.

When you learn more than the students you are attempting to teach, it is a good thing. A teacher should strive to learn always. The day a teacher settles back into knowing it all is the day that teacher begins to self-destruct. It may take years or even decades, but we have all known a teacher like that. He or she knows more than anyone else and finds an excuse for everything that might imply he/she needs to change something. It will always be the students' fault that things are not going well in the classroom. The administration will be blamed for many things as well. Blame the school board, the parents, or even the schedule! The All-Knowing teacher is a pain to be around and will become someone who others wish would retire. This is not good. Always be the teacher who welcomes new ideas and teaching strategies. It is normal to be frustrated when folks who really know little about the classroom tell you what to do but what profession is not plagued by that? It is part of life, so learn to cope with it. Simply put: do not stay stagnant. Be current, but never let go of what works.

Chapter Twenty-two

Stretching yourself in ways
You would never expect

A year into my retirement, I was asked to direct a play for kids affected by autism. I really didn't have much of a reaction. I mean, after so many years in the classroom, working with a few special needs kids wasn't that far from my expertise. On the other hand, I did not have *any* experience with an entire cast with all sorts of autism issues. Piece of cake! I have been wrong many times in my career, but I was not prepared for just how wrong I was with this situation!

I decided to direct them in Shakespeare's *A Midsummer Night's Dream*, my favorite Shakespearean comedy. Armed with years of knowledge and experience with this play, I felt more than confident heading into auditions.

The students ranged in age from eight through adult. Some were severely affected and rarely spoke or made eye contact with anyone. Some were very active physically, play fighting or running around the room caught up in their own story unfolding inside their heads. One boy was almost asleep on the floor. One girl was texting on her cell phone. Another boy was walking around most deliberately, speaking softly to himself and stopping once in a while to acknowledge others. Still another was "stemming", repeatedly neighing like a horse as she pranced around the room.

I took a look, evaluated what I saw, and quickly shot one of those little "arrow prayers" straight up to God. You know the ones, where your eyes are open and you catch just enough breath to say, "Dear God, help me," before feeling like you are going to pass out.

I asked the students to sit down and to my delight, they did. Well, the sleeping boy remained on the floor, but his aide eventually coaxed him into a chair. I introduced myself and invited them to tell me something about themselves that I could not know by just looking at them. I found them to be most interesting and entertaining. Within a few minutes, I was being educated in the most delightful way about this unusual behavior called autism.

As my auditions and subsequent rehearsals continued, I found my time spent with these students to be enlightening and positive. Basically, I fell in love with them. They were bright, capable, witty, and engaged-for the most part. Unlike their "normal" peers, they did not talk back, argue or complain. They memorized quickly and accurately. Where problems arose with focus or communication, the aides and I worked to pull them around to the job at hand. And always, always, most were kind, sweet, and wanted reassurance. I would get a hand on my shoulder or a pat on my arm, and I translated that to mean I was accepted and okay. Either that or they were trying to help me relax among them, and they were concerned for me. A reversal of roles.

We performed the show and I was very proud of them. In spite of my fear that they would fall asleep on stage or miss their entrance altogether, the show did happen. I even breathed deeply and smiled when King Oberon put his hand on my shoulder backstage during Act V. He leaned down to me where I was sitting at my stage manager desk, headset in place and script in front of me and calmly whispered, "Judy, am I in this scene?" I answered back, "Yes...yes, you are." What was his calm reply? "Oh good. I like this scene."

Whatever fear or trepidation I felt at the beginning melted away, and I saw these students in a light of respect and awe. They had issues with communication, yet they spoke lines one after the other, not just modern dialogue, but Shakespeare. They entered the stage on cue and did what they set out to do and with the best of their ability. Who could ask for more than that of ANY student? And who learned the most from the experience? Me, of course. I will forever see Titania, Queen of the Fairies, with her stuffed Yoda from Star Wars and remember my Puck, who took on the role so he could support his autistic brother. This was Shakespeare as I had never seen, but somehow, I am sure William himself would have smiled.

Chapter Twenty-three

A normal middle school day
or
In truth there are no normal days

I have always waivered between jealousy and relief when I looked at other professions and what their days are like. I find it interesting that many jobs take place in a quiet office where one meets with one or two folks at a time. Where "lunch hour" really means an hour and where you put your purse in a drawer, unlocked and it will stay safe.

Some jobs have set hours with no need to take work home. Some jobs do not require you to become emotionally involved with the success of your clients. They enter your life, complete their business, and leave-perhaps for a week, a month, or perhaps forever. This is not the case with teaching, at least in a middle school. To survive the attitudes, rolling eyes, passive defiance, and reluctance to complete homework, the great teachers must be passionate about their work. This is not just a job. This is a huge investment in the future of our world. You have the power to take these pre-adolescents into a whole new place where they want to learn, even clamber to learn. Do your job right and you will be preparing extra-credit and enrichment materials for kids that before having you as a teacher, never wanted to do anything extra. Like magic, formerly disengaged students will be suddenly lapping it up, feeling very empowered.

But I digress. I was trying to prepare you for what a normal day is like in a middle school. It isn't. Middle school is so delightfully unexpected that you can expect it to be that way. I once counted twelve interruptions during a class. These were not notes from the office or emergencies, but all things that happened within the classroom. "I have to leave early for an orthodontic appointment," "I have to go to the office to take my allergy medicine," "I feel like I am going to throw up," "I think I just started my period," "I have something in my eye," "Do you know what this sticky stuff is that is on my desk?" "Something smells like dog poop," "John just farted. Can I move?" "I forgot my glasses and I can't see the board," " Do you have a pencil that I can borrow?"

There are others but you get the idea. It isn't about you or your lesson at those moments. It is all about them. Middle school students are obsessed with themselves. They have progressed from having a parent consumed with their every move and well-being to this middle ground where it is up to them to advocate for themselves and learn to make decisions. They know they are not really in control. They think they want to be and therefore will push for independence. The heat is on for them to perform as responsible almost-adults. Truth is, they *want* to be adult, but they have yet to master so many skills needed to make wise decisions and look ahead to possible consequences of their decisions.

While it is all about them, it is also all about their world. It most definitely is NOT about you, their teacher. Before arriving in *your* room for *your* lesson, a mountain of things may have happened to them. Some overslept, some didn't eat breakfast or even brush their teeth. Some forgot their notebook, just came from having their braces tightened, or couldn't get their locker opened. There may have been harsh words between them and their parents, lunch forgotten on the kitchen counter at home, or a subtle harassment in the hall on their way to class. Some have been shoved in the hallway, tripped in front of others who laughed at them, and others caught running in the hall and had to listen to a teacher reprimand them. In the eyes of a middle schooler, these events, which may seem minor to an adult, are close to the apocalypse for them. As a teacher who cares for them, it is my duty to understand that behavior. This is not rocket science, but as a successful teacher, one must have a sixth sense and be able to understand their world to adjust the lesson for optimum value. Another thing that happens *to* them is their bodies. Most would see the natural changes that shout out to the world that they are no longer children as normal, "no big deal" happenings, but to a 13-year-old, it is happening to them and to them alone.

So, a normal day in middle school just doesn't happen. Don't expect it to, and you will not be disappointed. Little did I know then what I now know. Teaching is a lot like most things in life, like having children or grandchildren. Just about the time you think you have it figured out, either the "rules" change or the people simply choose not to follow your plan. I credit teaching middle school with helping me be a successful mother and grandmother. In fact, my eldest daughter once said to me, "Mom, it really isn't fair having you for a mom because you always know what I shouldn't do even before I do it." I think in a way it was a compliment, but she was correct. I got into the habit of thinking things out all the way to the possible endings and could usually sidestep any disastrous issues. Being a teacher makes you expect days that are topsy-turvy, and to even welcome them head-on.

Chapter Twenty-four

Teaching well means
Never having to make excuses

I have come to believe that I use excuses most often
when I am 1) not prepared, 2) feeling inadequate, or 3)
feeling jealous of what others have. Excuses crop up as a
smokescreen to hide my insecurities. When things are going
my way, I find no need for them.

Teachers are fallible human beings, and we teach
fallible human being *students*. Right there, the combination
is wrought with questionable possibilities. Seems we would
be far more successful if the students were, well, better.
Wait! Is that an excuse in the making? My point is that I
have listened and sadly, sometimes joined in with the art of
excuse making when things were not going well. As I
conclude these pages, I would be remiss if I didn't address
this topic.

I have taught in schools with few amenities and those
with plenty. I have taught in rooms designed for subjects
other than what I was teaching (lying on the floor in a smelly,
warm gymnasium just doesn't quite promote the inspired

writing and literature discussions I prefer), taught in carpeted rooms, those without carpet, rooms with clanging heaters from another era, and rooms with no windows. There have been rooms with broken desks, graffiti-decorated tabletops, no storage, heat that would not subside, rooms so cold I had to wear my coat and gloves all day, and on it goes.

I have taught students on welfare, some with parents in jail, some who miss school for exotic trips, those who have many special needs with no aides to assist, hungry students, students on drugs, and again, the list is never-ending. Don't even get me started on the two union strikes!

So what's the point? It can never be, "poor me," yet I heard plenty of that in my nearly four decades. The whining teacher will never win her battle with excuses. All it serves is frustration from a public that cares little for the complaints. My father used to say to me when I was little, "Stop your crying, or I will GIVE you something to cry about." I have remembered that edict my entire life. For me, it has come down to this: Speak up when there are safety issues in the classroom or you learn of a student in danger. Then, do what you can to get help and get it quickly. For everything else, just keep on keepin' on. Focus on the lesson and students in your room and just "get 'er done."

If you believe that you have an important job and you stay convinced, little else matters. Oh, I know how awful it feels as the class sizes go up, you are expected to do more work at home and your district keeps taking paid days out of your contract. These are real problems and concerns. They are not "fair" (whatever that means.) In a perfect world, these things should not be happening, but this takes us back to the fact that nothing is perfect. Not we teachers. Not the students. Not our classrooms. Not our contracts.

Use your gifts and remember that you are touching the future with your lessons. You have no way of knowing at that moment what impact you are making on that student. Author, mentor, and friend Bob Welch often quotes James Foley's poem which reads:

> Drop a pebble in the water;
> Just a splash and it is gone;
> But there's a half-a-hundred ripples
> Circling on and on,
> Spreading, spreading from the center,
> Flowing on out to the sea

And there's no way of telling
Where the end is going to be.

As the teacher, you are that pebble. You will cause thousands of ripples before you retire. You may never know what impact you had on your students, but trust me, you will have impacted them in some way. If you are fortunate, you will have students who choose to keep in contact with you the rest of your life. You will attend their weddings, celebrate the birth of their babies, weep with them as sorrow enters their lives, and be a part of their lives even from a distance and perhaps only through social media.

You have a very important job to do, and making excuses only serves as a distraction from the important task at hand. Take in all the information from the school board, administration, state, and district and then get on with the job of educating. You are the expert. You are investing in your students, and they are the winners. You can do this. With passion, humor, sternness, and love, you WILL do it. And there will be no excuses.

The End

My classroom was full of student mementos and gifts. A classroom should be a haven of inspiration and comfort. Make your room a place where kids *want* to hang out. Not only will it benefit them, it gives the teacher a valuable avenue to hear what is going on around the school. After all, they are out and about. It is the teacher who is isolated. Draw them in and be amazed at what you learn!

177

Another point being made. This time while I was
battling cancer. I had to keep laughing. The more cheerful I
was, the more my students cared and their concern returned
to encourage me.

This costume represents a lesson on proofreading which I wore one Halloween. I tried to get my point across about the importance of looking carefully at their writing. One little error–yes, even in spacing–changes what you are trying to say.

Former student Hannah Miller pictured as Belle in *Beauty and the Beast* was inspiring to her classmates as well as to my only two granddaughters at that time. Gifted students need to be encouraged as much as others. Sometimes we "lose" the gifted because they are not challenged. Raise the bar!

When you are passionate about middle schoolers, you find yourself among them, no matter where you are. Here, while travelling in Greece, we happened upon kids practicing their school program in an open-air theatre. They invited us to stay and watch. Except for the language and the teacher smoking, I could not tell the difference between these students and the American ones. Note the boy in the back with his cell phone.
Just the same...

Teaching as a guest teacher in Sydney, New South Wales in 2012. These students were introduced to Shakespeare by having fun with Puck's final speech in *A Midsummer Night's Dream*. The key to their enjoyment was a very short presentation by me and having them up and moving for the remainder of the class. They enjoyed group work and the freedom to present in a way that was comfortable for them. Some acted, some danced, some narrated.

As emcee of the yearly Eugene Education Foundation fundraiser, I had the joy of wearing the "ass'" head I had made for my productions of *A Midsummer Night's Dream.* It got the adults' attention just the same as it did the students'. This non-profit organization was founded to replace funds lost by changing taxes and other revenue. This is always a concern for teachers, especially with the arts since they are most often cut in spite of their importance. Teachers will do most anything to ensure their students have what they need to succeed. That includes looking like an _ _ _.

Made in the USA
San Bernardino, CA
12 October 2013